MW01065280

THOMAS
MERTON

SPIRITUAL LEADERS AND THINKERS

MARY BAKER EDDY

MOHANDAS GANDHI

AYATOLLAH RUHOLLAH KHOMEINI

MARTIN LUTHER

AIMEE SEMPLE McPHERSON

THOMAS MERTON

DALAI LAMA (TENZIN GYATSO)

SPIRITUAL
LEADERS AND
THINKERS

THOMAS
MERTON

Samuel Willard Crompton

Introductory Essay by
Martin E. Marty, Professor Emeritus
University of Chicago Divinity School

CHELSEA HOUSE
PUBLISHERS
A Haights Cross Communications Company

P h i l a d e l p h i a

CHELSEA HOUSE PUBLISHERS

VP, NEW PRODUCT DEVELOPMENT   Sally Cheney
DIRECTOR OF PRODUCTION   Kim Shinners
CREATIVE MANAGER   Takeshi Takahashi
MANUFACTURING MANAGER   Diann Grasse

Staff for THOMAS MERTON

EXECUTIVE EDITOR   Lee Marcott
SENIOR EDITOR   Tara Koellhoffer
PRODUCTION EDITOR   Megan Emery
ASSISTANT PHOTO EDITOR   Noelle Nardone
SERIES AND COVER DESIGNER   Keith Trego
LAYOUT   21st Century Publishing and Communications, Inc.

A Haights Cross Communications Company

www.chelseahouse.com

First Printing

9 8 7 6 5 4 3 2 1

Library of Congress Cataloging-in-Publication Data applied for.

ISBN 0-7910-7862-0

CONTENTS

Foreword

Why become acquainted with notable people when making efforts to understand the religions of the world?

Most of the faith communities number hundreds of millions of people. What can attention paid to one tell about more, if not most, to say nothing of *all*, their adherents? Here is why:

The people in this series are exemplars. If you permit me to take a little detour through medieval dictionaries, their role will become clear.

In medieval lexicons, the word *exemplum* regularly showed up with a peculiar definition. No one needs to know Latin to see that it relates to "example" and "exemplary." But back then, *exemplum* could mean something very special.

That "ex-" at the beginning of such words signals "taking out" or "cutting out" something or other. Think of to "excise" something, which is to snip it out. So, in the more interesting dictionaries, an *exemplum* was referred to as "a clearing in the woods," something cut out of the forests.

These religious figures are *exempla*, figurative clearings in the woods of life. These clearings and these people perform three functions:

First, they define. You can be lost in the darkness, walking under the leafy canopy, above the undergrowth, plotless in the pathless forest. Then you come to a clearing. It defines with a sharp line: there, the woods end; here, the open space begins.

Great religious figures are often stumblers in the dark woods.

We see them emerging in the bright light of the clearing, blinking, admitting that they had often been lost in the mysteries of existence, tangled up with the questions that plague us all, wandering without definition. Then they discover the clearing, and, having done so, they point our way to it. We then learn more of who we are and where we are. Then we can set our own direction.

Second, the *exemplum*, the clearing in the woods of life, makes possible a brighter vision. Great religious pioneers in every case experience illumination and then they reflect their light into the hearts and minds of others. In Buddhism, a key word is *enlightenment*. In the Bible, "the people who walked in darkness have seen a great light." They see it because their prophets or savior brought them to the sun in the clearing.

Finally, when you picture a clearing in the woods, an *exemplum*, you are likely to see it as a place of cultivation. Whether in the Black Forest of Germany, on the American frontier, or in the rain forests of Brazil, the clearing is the place where, with light and civilization, residents can cultivate, can produce culture. As an American moviegoer, my mind's eye remembers cinematic scenes of frontier days and places that pioneers hacked out of the woods. There, they removed stones, planted, built a cabin, made love and produced families, smoked their meat, hung out laundered clothes, and read books. All that can happen in clearings.

In the case of these religious figures, planting and cultivating and harvesting are tasks in which they set an example and then inspire or ask us to follow. Most of us would not have the faintest idea how to find or be found by God, to nurture the Holy Spirit, to create a philosophy of life without guidance. It is not likely that most of us would be satisfied with our search if we only consulted books of dogma or philosophy, though such may come to have their place in the clearing.

Philosopher Søren Kierkegaard properly pointed out that you cannot learn to swim by being suspended from the ceiling on a belt and reading a "How To" book on swimming. You learn because a parent or an instructor plunges you into water, supports you when necessary, teaches you breathing and motion, and then releases you to swim on your own.

Kierkegaard was not criticizing the use of books. I certainly have nothing against books. If I did, I would not be commending this series to you, as I am doing here. For guidance and courage in the spiritual quest, or—and this is by no means unimportant!—in intellectual pursuits, involving efforts to understand the paths others have taken, there seems to be no better way than to follow a fellow mortal, but a man or woman of genius, depth, and daring. We "see" them through books like these.

Exemplars come in very different styles and forms. They bring differing kinds of illumination, and then suggest or describe diverse patterns of action to those who join them. In the case of the present series, it is possible for someone to repudiate or disagree with *all* the religious leaders in this series. It is possible also to be nonreligious and antireligious and therefore to disregard the truth claims of all of them. It is more difficult, however, to ignore them. Atheists, agnostics, adherents, believers, and fanatics alike live in cultures that are different for the presence of these people. "Leaders and thinkers" they may be, but most of us do best to appraise their thought in the context of the lives they lead or have led.

If it is possible to reject them all, it is impossible to affirm everything that all of them were about. They disagree with each other, often in basic ways. Sometimes they develop their positions and ways of thinking by separating themselves from all the others. If they met each other, they would likely judge each other cruelly. Yet the lives of each and all of them make a contribution to the intellectual and spiritual quests of those who go in ways other than theirs. There are tens of thousands of religions in the world, and millions of faith communities. Every one of them has been shaped by founders and interpreters, agents of change and prophets of doom or promise. It may seem arbitrary to walk down a bookshelf and let a finger fall on one or another, almost accidentally. This series may certainly look arbitrary in this way. Why precisely the choice of these exemplars?

In some cases, it is clear that the publishers have chosen someone who has a constituency. Many of the world's 54 million Lutherans may be curious about where they got their name, who the man Martin Luther was. Others are members of a community but choose isolation: The hermit monk Thomas Merton is typical. Still others are exiled and achieve their work far from the clearing in which they grew up; here the Dalai Lama is representative. Quite a number of the selected leaders had been made unwelcome, or felt unwelcome in the clearings, in their own childhoods and youth. This reality has almost always been the case with women like Mary Baker Eddy or Aimee Semple McPherson. Some are extremely controversial: Ayatollah Ruhollah Khomeini stands out. Yet to read of this life and thought as one can in this series will be illuminating in much of the world of conflict today.

Reading of religious leaders can be a defensive act: Study the lives of certain ones among them and you can ward off spiritual—and sometimes even militant—assaults by people who follow them. Reading and learning can be a personally positive act: Most of these figures led lives that we can indeed call exemplary. Such lives can throw light on communities of people who are in no way tempted to follow them. I am not likely to be drawn to the hermit life, will not give up my allegiance to medical doctors, or be successfully nonviolent. Yet Thomas Merton reaches me and many non-Catholics in our communities; Mary Baker Eddy reminds others that there are more ways than one to approach healing; Mohandas Gandhi stings the conscience of people in cultures like ours where resorting to violence is too frequent, too easy.

Finally, reading these lives tells something about how history is made by imperfect beings. None of these subjects is a god, though some of them claimed that they had special access to the divine, or that they were like windows that provided for illumination to that which is eternal. Most of their stories began with inauspicious childhoods. Sometimes they were victimized, by parents or by leaders of religions from which they later broke.

Some of them were unpleasant and abrasive. They could be ungracious toward those who were near them and impatient with laggards. If their lives were symbolic clearings, places for light, many of them also knew clouds and shadows and the fall of night. How they met the challenges of life and led others to face them is central to the plot of all of them.

I have often used a rather unexciting concept to describe what I look for in books: *interestingness*. The authors of these books, one might say, had it easy, because the characters they treat are themselves so interesting. But the authors also had to be interesting and responsible. If, as they wrote, they would have dulled the personalities of their bright characters, that would have been a flaw as marring as if they had treated their subjects without combining fairness and criticism, affection and distance. To my eye, and I hope in yours, they take us to spiritual and intellectual clearings that are so needed in our dark times.

Martin E. Marty
The University of Chicago

1

The Choice

*I had wondered what was holding the
country together, what has been keeping the
universe from cracking in pieces and falling apart.*
—Merton's Journals, 1941

The world was a troubled place in the spring of 1941. Adolf Hitler's Nazi war machine had conquered France and the Netherlands the previous year, and had narrowly missed winning the Battle for Britain in the skies. British Prime Minister Winston Churchill spoke of the Royal Air Force pilots when he said that "never before has so much been owed by so many to so few." Now, in the early spring, Hitler's armies appeared ready to strike once more. No one knew just where the blow would fall.

Americans awaited news from Europe with anxiety. Millions of Americans were descended from English, French, Dutch, or other European ancestors; the people who had received Hitler's blows were their distant relatives. Millions of Americans were Germans; they could not be indifferent to the madness that had overtaken their former nation, or the dangers to which Hitler would expose their motherland. Everywhere, Americans were anxious.

At St. Bonaventure College in upstate New York, there was an English instructor who suffered both from the anxieties of the time and from a set of deeply personal concerns. He was twenty-six-year-old Thomas Merton, the son of a father from New Zealand and an American mother (Merton proudly claimed Welsh descent for both of his parents).

Merton had been in and around New York City for a number of years. His maternal grandparents had lived on the western part of Long Island, and he had had the good fortune to be able to spend some of his youth in a carefree fashion. He had then thought better of his behavior, converted to Catholicism, and become a strict observer of the faith. Now, in early 1941, he felt listless and bored. His writing was not going as well as he had hoped. On March 18, he described his latest experience with a publisher; this one was the *New Yorker* magazine, already famous as the one whose literary style was to be imitated by so many others:

> The first insult of the day, after getting off the five-thirty train into the freezing storm, was when I found the letter from the *New Yorker* saying my poem containing a parody on "Beauty

is truth, etc. . . . ” was a parody of Emily Dickinson and their readers would mostly be unfamiliar with that poem “of hers” so they couldn’t use it.

I never read a line of Emily Dickinson.

Now I really think I shouldn’t send anything more to them.[1]

Merton was, as we might say, “down in the dumps” or “down on his luck.” In several years of writing for magazines and writing novels, he had experienced off-again, on-again success, but the receipt of letters like this one had a dampening effect on his spirit. Certainly he was not much different from other writers in 1941; they all knew how keen the competition was, and how many articles the magazines received. Just the same, Merton regarded this letter as an “insult.”

Merton was feeling that modern life was much less valuable than it should be. Maybe he would try moving somewhere else, and see if there was something better. Just a few weeks later, he was on a train, bound for the remote location of the Abbey of Gethsemani in central Kentucky. Merton had heard about the Order of Trappist monks at Gethsemani, and he hoped to learn something about them. Once or twice in the past he had flirted with the idea of being a monk or a priest, but he had been turned down by the Franciscan Order. Now he went to Gethsemani. His journal entry for April 7, 1941, is one of the most poignant he ever wrote:

I should tear out all the other pages of this book and all the other pages of everything else I ever wrote, and begin here.

This is the center of America. I had wondered what was holding the country together, what has been keeping the universe from cracking in pieces and falling apart. It is this monastery if only this one. (There must be two or three others.) . . .

This is the only real city in America—in a desert.

It is the axle around which the whole country blindly turns.

> Washington is paint and plaster and noise-making machines and lunacy: this country hasn't got a capital or a heart or any focal point to it except Gethsemani.[2]

Even for Thomas Merton, who had long been skillful with the written word, these were powerful statements to make. What had he found at Gethsemani that had been lacking in the many other places he had been—including France, England, Italy, and New York City?

The answer did not come right away. In spite of his remarkable enthusiasm for the place, Merton stayed only one week, as a guest of the monastery. Ten days later, he was back at St. Bonaventure College, teaching and writing feverishly. Something at Gethsemani had touched his soul, but he was not yet certain that he had a calling to the life of the Trappist monks.

Founded in France in the eleventh century, the Trappist Order is perhaps the most rigorous of all monastic groups. Trappist monks, following the rule of St. Benedict, take vows of obedience, stability, and conversion of manners (which includes poverty and chastity). They do not leave the grounds except in the case of medical emergencies. So, what called to Merton that April day in 1941 was the opportunity to drop out of the secular world completely, to become "dead" to the outside world. He had found one of the few places in North America where a seeker could become a finder in the medieval tradition.

He was not yet certain, though, and he was not yet ready. During the summer and early fall of 1941, Merton pondered two possibilities. The first was, of course, to apply to enter the monastery of Gethsemani; the second possibility was to do charity work among the poor in New York City's Harlem neighborhood. Merton had recently made a friend of Catherine de Hueck, a Russian baroness who had fled her native land at the time of its Communist revolution in 1917. The baroness had become an ardent worker for the poor, and had started a settlement house in Harlem. Merton also had numerous friends and a former professor—the classicist Mark Van Doren—who urged him to try another possibility: to make writing his full-time vocation. Merton struggled with the different choices, and as summer gave way to autumn, his thoughts were rich with despair:

> I have been happy here [at St. Bonaventure] in a way, but never content, never completely at rest in the sense that this was where I belonged. . . .
>
> All the arguments against going are jokes—transparently easy to see through, since they are all denied by the Gospels, the Beatitudes, the Baroness herself in asking me, and by me myself, who really desire no other thing than this which I have been praying for ceaselessly since August: that I may give myself entirely to God's service!
>
> Before I had given the Baroness the first argument (about writing) I realized how foolish all the arguments would be.
>
> That I am meant to stay here and write!
>
> That I am meant to stay here and teach!
>
> That I am meant to stay here and pray and meditate a lot![3]

THE BARONESS

Sometime in 1941, Merton made the acquaintance of Catherine de Hueck. Born in Russia in 1896, she was a Russian aristocrat. Her father's career meant that the family traveled a good deal, and she studied at a Catholic school in Egypt in her teens. There, she developed the idea that she wanted to make a bridge between the Eastern Orthodox Church and Roman Catholicism.

The Russian Revolution of 1917 threw all her plans askew. She and her husband emigrated first to Canada, and then to the United States. She divorced her husband, and became an ardent worker for poverty relief. She founded the first Friendship House in Toronto, Canada, and the second in Harlem in 1938. That was where she and Merton met in 1941.

The baroness married a reporter named Eddie Doherty in 1943. The couple moved to Canada in 1947, where she founded the Madonna House in Combermere, Ontario. Like Thomas Merton, she was extremely prolific, writing more than twenty books in her lifetime.

The more he pondered the arguments against going to Gethsemani, the weaker they sounded to his analytical brain.

Even as he wrestled with the decision, Merton was plugging away at his next piece of writing. In the summer and early autumn of 1941, he wrote *Journal of My Escape from the Nazis*, which was published many years later as *My Argument with the Gestapo: A Macaronic Journal*. In the preface to this book, Merton described his only encounter with the supporters of Hitler in Nazi Germany:

> One Sunday morning in the spring of 1932 I was hiking through the Rhine Valley. With a pack on my back I was wandering down a quiet country road among flowering apple orchards, near Koblenz. Suddenly a car appeared and came down the road very fast. It was jammed with people. Almost before I had taken full notice of it, I realized it was coming straight at me and instinctively jumped into the ditch. The car passed in a cloud of leaflets and from the ditch I glimpsed its occupants, six or seven youths screaming and shaking their fists. They were Nazis, and it was election day. I was being invited to vote for Hitler, who was not yet in power. These were future officers in the SS. They vanished quickly. The road was once again perfectly silent and peaceful. But it was not the same road as before. It was now a road on which seven men had expressed their readiness to destroy me.[4]

Merton went on to mock both the Nazi regime and the futile efforts of England, France, and others to contain the threat. In his work, there was also, even at this early stage, a thread of pacifism and a belief in nonviolence that would later become stronger.

We do not know the exact moment at which Merton decided to leave New York. But he ended his private journals on December 5 of that year, and was on a train headed south on December 9. In between those two dates one of the most memorable events in American history occurred: the Japanese attack on the naval base at Pearl Harbor, Hawaii.

Merton was not oblivious to the events of World War II. He had listened to the radio with horror as his native France succumbed to the Germans, and he was even more agonized to learn that London—where he spent part of his youth—had been bombed by German planes. Early in 1941, Merton had received a possible draft notice, but his bad teeth (he had perennial problems with them) had almost ensured that he would not be accepted for duty. Then, late in November, came another notice informing him that men with bad teeth were now eligible, and he might be called to serve.

Merton did not shrink from the thought of going to war. Self-preservation was never one of his highest priorities; he had more of the poet and the romantic in him than the practical person. He had already made an internal resolution that if he were drafted, he would indeed serve in the military, but he would never kill anyone, for any reason. Having made that decision, he felt free to accelerate his choice to apply to the monastery, which would be a way to fulfill the medieval conception of how to attain closeness with God.

Merton gave away all of his personal effects and nearly all of his books. Letters, books, diaries, and the drafts of novels all went to Mark Van Doren and eventually ended up in the archives of St. Bonaventure College. Merton left St. Bonaventure on December 9, 1941.

Years later, Merton described his arrival at Gethsemani:

> I rang the bell at the gate. It let fall a dull, unresonant note inside the empty court. My man got in his car and went away. Nobody came. I could hear somebody moving around inside the Gatehouse. I did not ring again. Presently, the window opened, and Brother Matthew looked out between the bars, with his clear eyes and graying beard.
>
> "Hullo, Brother," I said.
>
> He recognized me, glanced at the suitcase and said: "This time have you come to stay?"

"Yes Brother, if you'll pray for me," I said.

Brother nodded, and raised his hand to close the window.

"That's what I've been doing," he said, "praying for you."[5]

Merton had many friends in New York, who mourned his departure. His literary agent, Naomi Burton, learned from one of his closest friends that a Trappist monk was allowed to write only a few letters a year, and that these were restricted to the length of half a page. "Oh God! He'll never write again!"

It was too early to mourn. Merton was off on a grand adventure, and his pen would blossom again in the future.

2

From Prades to Cambridge

*The more you try to avoid suffering, the more you suffer,
because smaller and more insignificant things begin to
torture you, in proportion to your fear of being hurt.*
—Thomas Merton, *The Seven Storey Mountain*

Thomas Merton was born on January 31, 1915, at Prades in southern France. His father, Owen Merton, came from New Zealand, while his mother, Ruth Jenkins, was an American. Merton's parents were from separate parts of the world, and he spent his first year in France, to which neither of his parents properly belonged. They had gone to southern France for the scenery, which Owen Merton featured in some of his many paintings.

Truly, Thomas Merton was born to a family of artists rather than a family of spiritual seekers. He later described his father's unarticulated faith as a strong one, but it was entirely uninformed by any religious tradition. Both of his parents had come of age in a time of considerable optimism about the future, and they, along with many of their contemporaries, saw less need for God. This changed, of course, with the start of the Great War (later called World War I) in 1914. As Merton later put it, "Not many hundreds of miles away from the house where I was born, they were picking up the men who rotted in the rainy ditches among the dead horses and the ruined seventy-fives, in a forest of trees without branches along the river Marne."[6]

The Battle of the Marne is not very well known today, but for Europeans of 1914 and 1915 it had a tragic connotation. Perhaps three-quarters of a million men—British, French, and German—had lost their lives in the terrible fight for the Marne River, which governed the approaches to Paris.

Happily, young Merton knew nothing of this. He was indeed an aware child, but even his capacious memory would not stretch back to these times. What we know of his infancy comes from the pen of his mother. She seems to have been influenced by the modern theories of child raising, and she wrote down virtually every possible detail, so she could eventually show the logbook to Owen's mother in New Zealand. Thus, we know that Merton was both alert and enormously active from his first months. Interestingly, he showed little interest in toys of any kind, and was attracted instead to books. His mother recorded that, "When we go out he seems conscious of everything. Sometimes he puts up his arms and cries out 'Oh sun! Oh joli!' Often it is to the birds or trees that he makes these pagan hymns of joy."[7]

Knowing as we do that Merton became a lifelong devotee of nature, we might think that his mother was influenced by his later behavior when she recorded these incidents. But she died long before young Thomas became an adult, so we can only look at her words as something of a prophecy about his later character.

When Merton was just about one year old, the small family packed up and left France. It had become increasingly difficult for Owen Merton, who was in the awkward position of being a New Zealander in France, yet not serving in the army of either of those nations. The family crossed the Atlantic in a steamship and settled in Douglaston, New York, at the home of Merton's maternal grandparents. There he was exposed to influences quite different from those of small-town France.

His grandfather, Samuel Jenkins, was known throughout the family simply as "Pop." His grandmother, Martha Baldwin Jenkins, was known as "Bonnemaman." The couple made a striking contrast to one another. Pop was ambitious, gregarious, and sometimes outlandish, while his wife was demure and retiring. Pop had made a small fortune working in publishing for Grosset and Dunlap. He was one of the first to see that motion pictures held the potential to increase book sales rather than force them to decline, and Pop and the family were ardent devotees of the new silent films. Merton later claimed that he and his brother saw virtually all the films that came out between 1934 and 1937.

Young Merton enjoyed the change of scenery, and probably basked in the love his doting grandparents showed him. They were delighted to have him on their side of the Atlantic, and wanted their daughter and son-in-law to enjoy a comfortable middle-class life in the United States. There was only one problem: Owen Merton was far too independent to follow in the path of his father-in-law. Owen continued to paint, and even when he failed to make a decent living for his family, he nevertheless rejected any further assistance from his father-in-law.

The Mertons spent some time in Maryland, then went back to Douglaston. In 1918, Ruth Merton had a second child. Thomas Merton noticed that his new younger brother, John Paul, had a much gentler and more serene nature than his own: "I remember that everyone was impressed by his constant and unruffled happiness. In the long evenings, when he was put to bed before the sun went down, instead of protesting and fighting, as I did when I had to go to bed, he would lie upstairs in his crib, and we would hear him singing a little tune."[8]

The Merton boys lost their mother to cancer in 1921. During her illness, she made every effort to appear as if things were normal, and the boys were exposed to the truth only at the end. Merton later described the painful scene in his autobiographical *The Seven Storey Mountain*:

> My grandparents did not have a car, but they hired one to go in to the hospital, when the end finally came. I went with them in the car, but was not allowed to enter the hospital. Perhaps it was just as well. What would have been the good of my being plunged into a lot of naked suffering and emotional crisis without any prayer, any Sacrament to stabilize and order it, and make some kind of meaning out of it? In that sense, Mother was right. Death, under those circumstances, was nothing but ugliness, and if it could not possibly have any ultimate meaning, why burden a child's mind with the sight of it?[9]

In the following years, Merton's younger brother was left with the grandparents, but Merton himself went with his father, first to Bermuda, where they stayed a short while, and then back to France. It was not quite the France they had left almost ten years earlier. The Great War was now over, and even though life had once again become as normal as possible, the fact always loomed that between one and two million young Frenchmen had lost their lives in the conflict.

Father and son did not return to Prades, but moved instead to St. Antonin, another town in south-central France. Owen Merton often left his young son with friends while he went off to paint landscape scenes. One of Merton's finest and most touching memories comes from a middle-aged French couple who cared for him temporarily while his father was away. Merton describes them as sturdy peasants, utterly devoted to each other and their land, and without concerns for or knowledge of the wider world. Theirs, he claimed, was perhaps the first unselfish love he had received. They asserted no claim with their love; they simply cared for Thomas in a deep and wonderful way, and he felt sure that they were saints in disguise.

Merton's elementary school days were a mixture of pleasure and pain. He was teased unmercifully by his classmates for his English accent, and he got into numerous scuffles. We know little about Merton in these days, but our knowledge is enhanced by the recollections of George Linieres, one of his classmates:

> My friends and I found him somewhat peculiar because he wasn't dressed as we were at that time. So to us he was a stranger; we called him "the English boy," even though he was an American. I still remember he was wearing pants that we'd never seen before, knickerbockers. He was also wearing some strange shoes. They were what we wear now, baskets. We were about seven or eight years behind America in those days; now, thanks to the media, we're not so far behind.[10]

Linieres also recalled Merton as a student:

> Thomas was considered to be a little prodigy at St. Antonin because in one or two years he learned what it took others three or four years to learn. He was, according to my instructor, my friend M. Gagnot, the best student he ever had in French. He got the best grades. So you see, his vocation as a writer had begun back then.[11]

Owen Merton's painting improved during the 1920s, and he

had even less time to spend with Thomas. Father and son moved to England in 1928, and young Merton was left with relatives in England while Owen Merton painted, having had a successful exhibition in London in 1925. Just as Owen Merton's fortunes improved, however, his health took a sharp turn for the worse. While young Merton attended Oakham school, his father was diagnosed with a malignant brain tumor.

Young Merton did well at Oakham. His studies were generally easy for him, and his greatest challenge was to stay out of trouble. He retained the incredible vigor and drive his mother had once observed, and he needed all sorts of occupations, including rugby and rowing, to stay in bounds. Meanwhile, his father's condition deteriorated, and in the summer of 1930, Merton went to visit his father in the hospital. He found him unable to speak: "The sorrow of his great helplessness suddenly fell upon me like a mountain. I was crushed by it. The tears sprang to my eyes. Nobody said anything more."[12]

Merton had been very young when his mother passed away, and her death had not affected him in the same way that his father's now did. Merton reflected upon the pity and shame of it all:

> What could I make of so much suffering? There was no way for me, or for anyone else in the family, to get anything out of it. It was a raw wound for which there was no adequate relief. You had to take it, like an animal. We were in the condition of most of the world, the condition of men without faith in the presence of war, disease, pain, starvation, suffering, plague, bombardment, death.[13]

Later, Merton described this as one of the turning points of his life, and one of the cornerstones of his spiritual philosophy:

> Indeed, the truth that many people never understand, until it is too late, is that the more you try to avoid suffering, the more you suffer, because smaller and more insignificant things begin to torture you, in proportion to your fear of

being hurt. The one who does most to avoid suffering is, in the end, the one who suffers most: and his suffering comes to him from things so little and so trivial that one can say that it is no longer objective at all.[14]

Owen Merton died in January 1931. The obituary in the *London Times* stated:

Mr. Merton was a water-colour painter of distinction, who, had he lived longer, would have earned a wide reputation. . . . His pictures displayed a sense of design and a delicacy of colour which reflected his love of the Chinese masters, together with a strength and individuality which bore witness to the originality and power of the artists mind.[15]

Thomas Merton was now on his own, at the age of sixteen, although he had a legal guardian, Tom Bennett, his godfather and an old friend of his father's.

Young Thomas Merton did not appear to be scarred by the events of the time. He celebrated his eighteenth birthday on January 31, 1933, and soon left London, headed for France and then Italy. He was a young man, very much alone in the world, and he hoped to enjoy the fruits of a holiday upon the occasion of his coming of age.

Merton had recently graduated from Oakham school. He had lived for some time with his godparents in London, and now needed a break from them and their very English home. Driven almost by a sense of destiny, he crossed the English Channel to France, and soon found himself in the south of France where he had been born.

About the time that he reached Avignon—the beautiful city on the Rhône River—Merton had run out of money. He wired his godparents, asking for assistance. They sent him money, but also sent a telegram that scolded Merton, reminding him that he had to keep a watchful eye on his finances and not be a burden to other people. Merton was humiliated. Sometime soon after he received the money he reminisced that, "I believed in the beautiful myth about having a good time so long as it does not hurt anybody else. You cannot live for your own pleasure and your own convenience without inevitably hurting and injuring the feelings and the interests of practically everybody you meet."[16]

Merton pushed on to the southern coast. With one or two exceptions, the towns of the French Riviera appealed neither to his imagination nor to his sense of adventure. He boarded another train, crossed the Italian Alps, and soon found himself in Florence, Italy. As a recent school graduate, and as a young man who spoke well in at least three languages, Merton fancied himself a humanist, and as such he thought he would be perfectly at home in Florence, the city of Michelangelo, Leonardo da Vinci, and other great Italian artists. But he found Florence cold—both physically and otherwise—and he pushed on for the great city of Rome instead.

Every writer, every artist, and every Westerner who wishes to contribute in some way to art, architecture, music, or philosophy, wants to see Rome at least once. There are the obvious attractions of the Roman Coliseum, the Pantheon, and the beautiful bridges. There is the wonderful food, served on every street corner, and there is the golden Roman sunlight, appreciated by every traveler from Lord Byron to T.S. Eliot. Merton was no exception. He had spent the last several years in England, and he welcomed the sunlight that replaced the clouds and storms he had often experienced in London.

But Merton also experienced a strange sense of dissatisfaction. If he was indeed in the very center of the Western world, and if he was among the works and the ruins of the great masters, why did he not feel more at peace, more at one with himself?

> Things were going on as they usually did with me. But after about a week—I don't know how it began—I found myself looking into churches rather than into ruined temples. Perhaps it was the frescoes on the wall of an old chapel—ruined too— at the foot of the Palatine, at the edge of the Forum, that first aroused my interest in another and a far different Rome.[17]

Old frescoes appeared, one after the other. Merton became particularly fascinated by some Byzantine art, created long after the heyday of the original Roman Empire. He found something much more vital and much more spiritual in these works:

> And now for the first time in my life I began to find out something of Who this Person was that men called Christ. It was obscure, but it was a true knowledge of Him, in some sense, truer than I knew and truer than I would admit. But it was in Rome that my conception of Christ was formed. It was there I first saw Him. . . .[18]

Merton left Rome a few weeks later. He went to the small Trappist monastery of Tre Fontane, south of the Tiber River. There, he sat under a eucalyptus tree and had the thought, "I should like to become a Trappist monk."

Years passed before this notion was fulfilled. At this point in his life, what matters most is that Merton was drawn to religion, drawn by the things and images of a past in which he would ultimately become more comfortable than he was in his own times. For the moment, however, he remained Thomas Merton, a young man in the still rather young twentieth century.

3

Accomplishment and Shame

With my blind appetites,
it was impossible that I should not rush
in and take a huge bite of this rotten fruit.
—Thomas Merton, *The Seven Storey Mountain*

That September of 1933, Merton was back in England. He entered Clare College at Cambridge University, his tuition and expenses paid for by a trust his grandfather had created. Tom Bennett remained his legal guardian. Bennett hoped that Merton would do well at Cambridge and eventually enter the British diplomatic service.

The early 1930s were a heady time to be at Cambridge. England was just emerging from the pain and desolation brought on by World War I, and there was a clear desire to escape from the recent past. The poetry of T.S. Eliot, the transplanted American, had just become popular among Cambridge undergraduates, who saw their Englishness in a whole new way. For them, Eliot's poetry spoke to both the heartbreak and losses experienced by their parents' generation, as well as the new freedoms to which they themselves aspired.

Merton was not a typical undergraduate. His uprooted childhood, which began in the second year of his life, made him more traveled—and one might say more cynical—than most of his fellows. But Merton plunged in just the same, eager to experience as much of life as possible. He joined the student newspaper, wrote essays and drew cartoons, applied himself to his studies, and engaged in all sorts of pranks. Not all of these were innocent or harmless, however; it was at Cambridge that Merton developed his tendency to break hearts.

Whether he was actually as heartless toward the girls as he described, Merton was certainly a rake. He was fascinated with all sorts of girls, and often brought home working-class types who turned off his fellow undergraduates. Merton certainly entertained more girls than his classmates did.

He had boundless energy and seemed able to do everything at once. He read some T.S. Eliot and some William Blake, and because of his remarkable glibness was able to pass himself off in class as well informed. Reading his autobiographical *The Seven Storey Mountain*, one receives the impression that he was active for about nineteen hours out of every twenty-four-hour day.

Each series of flirtations and pranks, however, seems to

have brought on a spell of remorse. Merton later described his bitter and painful feelings toward his experiences at Cambridge University:

> Perhaps to you the atmosphere of Cambridge is neither dark nor sinister. Perhaps you were never there except in May. You never saw anything but the thin Spring sun half veiled in the mists and blossoms of the gardens along the Backs, smiling on the lavender bricks and stones of Trinity and St. John's, or my own college, Clare.
>
> I am even willing to admit that some people might live there for three years, or even a lifetime, so protected that they never sense the sweet stench of corruption that is all around them—the keen, thick scent of decay that pervades every-thing and accuses with a terrible accusation the superficial youthfulness, the abounding undergraduate noise that fills those ancient buildings. But for me, with my blind appetites, it was impossible that I should not rush in and take a huge bite of this rotten fruit. The bitter taste is still with me after not a few years.[19]

Merton was frequently drunk, and certainly had a number of love affairs. What was most painful, and what took him many years to admit, was that he probably got a girl pregnant, and that her family and his legal guardian urged him to have nothing further to do with her or his yet-to-be-born child.[20]

Tom Bennett had, by 1934, decided to wash his hands of Merton. Bennett summoned Merton to London and demanded that the young man account for his conduct. Merton made a show of saying meekly that he had never intended to harm anyone, but it was all too late. Bennett informed Merton that he would never make a career in the British diplomatic service, and that Cambridge was therefore a waste of time. By the early autumn of 1934, Merton was headed to the United States, the second of his many homes.

Merton crashed down to earth at Douglaston, New York,

where he was warmly received by Pop and Bonnemaman. They had never lost faith in him, and he and his brother John Paul were all they had left to remind them of their beloved daughter. Merton made his home in Douglaston, but soon began to attend Columbia University in the heart of Manhattan. Much of the next three years of his life would be spent taking interminable train rides, some of which were enlivened by writing and reading, but others that seemed like a nightmare.

Columbia in 1934 was far more suitable for a person like Merton than Cambridge had been. The American undergraduates were both less sophisticated and more joyful than their English counterparts were, and Merton made friends readily. He preferred arriving at Columbia via the subway to walking through the oak groves of Cambridge, and he found the student life much more real. Just as important, he found one of his few real academic mentors at Columbia in the person of Mark Van Doren. The course was in English literature, a subject that Merton—given his recent experiences at Cambridge—might have been expected to avoid. But he found Van Doren a remarkable and refreshing change from the professors at Cambridge:

> Mark would come into the room and, without any fuss, would start talking about whatever was to be talked about. Most of the time he asked questions. His questions were very good, and if you tried to answer them intelligently, you found yourself saying excellent things that you did not know you knew, and that you had not, in fact, known before. He had "educed" them from you by his question. His classes were literally "education"—they brought things out of you, they made your mind produce its own explicit ideas. Do not think that Mark was simply priming his students with thoughts of his own, and then making the thought stick to their minds by getting them to give it back to him as their own. Far from it. What he did have was the gift of communicating to them something of his own vital

interest in things, something of his manner of approach: but the results were sometimes quite unexpected—and by that I mean good in a way that he had not anticipated, casting lights that he had not himself forseen.[21]

Van Doren and Merton became quite friendly. Merton had a way of endearing himself to good teachers, and the two men remained friends long after. But even as he thrilled to Van Doren's teaching style, Merton was reading in a far-ranging pattern on his own; he simply could not absorb enough knowledge.

The classics, especially French; psychology, both classical and self-help; books on nutrition and health—all these and more were added to Merton's reading list at a time when he also served on the student newspaper and contributed to the student yearbook. Merton also developed a side interest in drawing cartoons. A number of his yearbook pictures have survived; they show him as an openly sophisticated young man, with a flair for dress and manner, but the eager eyes betray the loneliness he still felt. All this activity was not bringing him any closer to true peace.

One could certainly ask: What was the hurry? Merton was only twenty-two. Why did he feel he had to achieve some type of quick spiritual solution when he had a long life ahead of him? Although Merton did not say so explicitly, there is a strong sense in his journals that he feared an early death. He had seen both his parents die, and had watched as the pieces of his childhood world had collapsed around him. The impatient tearing quality of his twenties seems to betray a fear that he would "miss out" on life in some fashion.

All the hurry and bustle caught up with him in 1936. While taking the Long Island Rail Road, Merton experienced what seems like a heart attack, or at least the sign of some type of heart trouble. He had trouble breathing and concentrating. He went quickly to a doctor, who urged him to give up some of his activities.[22] This seemed impossible to Merton, who nevertheless was about to stumble onto one of the first spiritual awakenings of his life.

It was around this time that Merton lost his grandparents. Pop died unexpectedly in the fall of 1936 and Bonnemaman a year later. Merton grieved Pop's passing, but took the loss of his grandmother more philosophically. He knew that his only close relative left in the world was his brother, John Paul, but the two brothers were separated by their different upbringings. Unlike Thomas, John Paul had enjoyed a relatively secure childhood living at Douglaston. The brothers were also at different colleges: Merton at Columbia and John Paul at Cornell.

The death of Pop appears to have accelerated Merton's desire to find some type of meaning in the world, where he had experienced so much loss. By the late 1930s, he had turned to Roman Catholicism.

Like many young people of his era, Merton had an inherent suspicion of Roman Catholicism. This dislike of the Catholic Church seems to have stemmed from the nineteenth century, during which the Church had resisted many of the advances made by scientists and intellectuals. The discoveries of Charles Darwin were rejected, as had been those of Galileo Galilei before him. For many young intellectuals, the Catholic Church stood for the worst type of backward thinking.

The Church was also not helped by the manner in which some priests resisted President Franklin Roosevelt's sometimes radical New Deal policies that were aimed to help the country regain economic strength during the Great Depression. Father Charles Coughlin of Detroit gathered a large radio audience that listened to him rail against the New Deal and socialism; Father Coughlin was portrayed in the press as being closer to Benito Mussolini, the Italian dictator, than to the Roosevelt administration in the United States. So, the combination of backward thinking and regressive politics made Merton and others dislike the Catholic Church. A Catholic, Alfred E. Smith, had run for president in 1928, and had been trounced by the Protestant Herbert Hoover.

Given his education in the British system, and the teaching he had been exposed to at Columbia, Merton would not be expected to seek out the Catholic Church. Some type of free-thought religion might have been expected to appeal to him—not a Church that demanded conformity and obedience.

Merton, however, lived in and through paradox all his life. By 1938, he had become interested in Catholicism, and in November of that year, he was accepted as a member of the Roman Catholic faith. His Columbia friends, who loyally came to the baptism, were nearly all Jewish. Merton later wrote:

> For now I had entered into the everlasting movement of that gravitation which is the very life and spirit of God: God's own gravitation towards the depths of His own infinite nature, His goodness without end. And God, that center Who is every-where, and whose circumference is nowhere, finding me, through incorporation with Christ, incorporated into this immense and tremendous gravitational movement which is love, which is the Holy Spirit, loved me.
>
> And He called out to me from His own immense depths.[23]

Things were still far from smooth. Merton continued to drink and socialize, but he did so with more of a sense that something else was possible. In 1939, he earned his master's degree in English from Columbia. But he still felt rootless—until he applied to the Franciscan Order in New York in 1939. He asked to be admitted as a novice, to take up the ways of the Friars Minor, the official name of the Franciscan order.

All seemed well. Merton was scheduled to join the Francis-cans, but he felt compelled to tell them about the girl and baby he had left in England. When he was told that the Order of Friars Minor was not for him, Merton was crushed.[24]

Merton had an appendectomy in the winter of 1939–1940 and had the opportunity to travel to Cuba for a recuperative holiday. On that island, which was still twenty years away from Fidel Castro's regime, Merton experienced the loosest and most joyful form of religion he had yet seen. It was Roman Catholicism, of course; virtually no other religion was practiced in Cuba. Merton described some of the scenes of everyday life in his journal:

> If you are eating in the dining room of the plaza, you share in the life of the whole city. Out through the arcade you can see, up against the sky, a winged muse just standing tiptoe on top of one of the cupolas of the National Theater. Below that, the trees of the central park: and everybody seems to be circulating all about you, although they do not literally go in and out of the tables where the diners sit, eating dishes savory of saffron or black beans.
>
> Food is profuse and cheap: as for the rest, if you don't have the money, you don't have to pay for it: it is everybody's, it overflows all over the streets: your gaiety is not private, it belongs to everybody else, because everybody else has given it to you in the first place. The more you look at the city and move in it, the more you love it, and the more love you take from it, the more you give back to it. . . . This sinful city of Havana is so constructed that you may read in it, if you know how to live in it, an analogy of the kingdom of heaven.[25]

Here, in Havana, Merton saw something close to what he wanted. He wanted to live in a place and a world where things circulated freely, where people were not bound by money, status, or possessions. He felt he was Latin in his soul. Though he had attended British and American schools, he had been raised in an artistic tradition by his father, and his earliest memories went back to Prades, France, and the sound of church bells. Though he remained a lonely intellectual, Merton yearned for a life in which communality was felt and expressed.

Merton returned to New York and in the fall of 1940 he got a job teaching at St. Bonaventure College. He taught in the academic year 1940–1941. From the start, he was a gifted teacher, bringing much of what he had learned from Mark Van Doren to his students. Merton was given room, board, and $45 a month, no small achievement for an academic in the late stages of the Great Depression.

Merton visited the Abbey of Gethsemani in the spring of 1941. From the time of that visit until December 1941, when he made the choice to enter the abbey, he was in torment over the contrast between the worlds of action and contemplation. Should he remain in Harlem and work with the poor? Or should he go to Kentucky and return, in a sense, to the Middle Ages? He chose the latter, and by mid-December of 1941, he was a novice monk at the abbey.

4

The Order of the Cistercians of the Strict Observance

*A monk is a man who has given up
everything in order to possess everything.*

—Thomas Merton, *The Waters of Siloe*

What was it that Merton had entered? What was the Order of the Cistercians, and what was the difference between those who practiced the Common Observance and those who followed the Strict Observance, who were also known as Trappists? The answers lie in the Middle Ages and in the manner that the order settled in North America.

Western monasticism has been given this description, by none other than Thomas Merton: "A monk is a man who has given up everything in order to possess everything. He is one who has abandoned desire in order to achieve the highest fulfillment of all desire. He has renounced his liberty in order to become free. He goes to war because he has found a kind of war that is peace." [26]

Later, when he addressed the specifics of the Trappists, Merton wrote:

> Is it any wonder that Trappist monasteries are places full of peace and contentment and joy? These men, who have none of the pleasures of the world, have all the happiness that the world is unable to find. Their silence is more eloquent than all the speeches of politicians and the noise of all the radios in America. Their smiles have more joy in them than has the laughter of thousands. When they raise their eyes to the hills or to the sky, they a see a beauty which other people do not know how to find. When they work in the fields and the forests, they seem to be tired and alone, but their hearts are at rest, and they are absorbed in a companionship that is tremendous, because it is three Persons in one infinite Nature, the One Who spoke the universe and draws it all back into Himself by His Love; the One from Whom all things came and to Whom all things return: and in Whom are all the beauty and substance and actuality of everything in the world that is real.[27]

Western monasticism may be said to have begun in the sixth century with the founding of an abbey at Monte Cassino,

Italy. Benedict of Nursia (later known as St. Benedict) organized a group of like-minded men into the first Western monastery (the Byzantine East had had monasteries since about the third century A.D.). St. Benedict established his *Rule*, later adopted by all Western monasteries. The key words were *stability*, *conversion of manners*, and *obedience*, but Benedict did not make the monastic life a painful one: He believed monks should have plenty of sleep, rest, and food.

St. Benedict's example became known as Benedictine monasticism. It flourished in Christian Europe for hundreds of years, but as the centuries passed, the *Rule* was less strictly observed and the lives of the monks became too comfortable, at least according to their critics. One of the reasons that each religious group (Benedictine, Cistercian, Franciscan, and Dominican, among others) would run into trouble was that each became successful materially over time, and it was possible for the monks to live in greater personal comfort.

The great Abbey of Cluny was founded in France in A.D. 909. The Cluniac monks wanted to reform the Benedictine Order, and they spread far and wide. Their great mother house at Cluny had hundreds of daughter houses, spread throughout France, Germany, and northern Italy. By the end of the eleventh century, the Cluniac monks had become so influential and successful that people called into question their separation from the world. And so, around 1098, the Order of Cistercians was born. As Merton described it:

> The ferment of monastic reform that had brought so many new communities into existence in the eleventh century culminated, in 1098, with the foundation of a monastery whose filiations would soon develop into one of the greatest contemplative orders in the Church. Citeaux is supposed to have taken its name from the reeds—*cistels*, in Burgundian patois—which abounded in the marshy woodland where its twenty-two founders came to settle on Palm Sunday, 1098. The land was not far from Dijon, and it

belonged to the Duke of Burgundy. He made no difficulties about ceding it to the austere colonists: it was practically useless to anybody in the world except penitent monks, and he happened to share the general respect for their abbot, Robert of Molesme.[28]

The Cistercians did not really want to separate themselves from Benedictine monasticism; rather, they insisted on a return to the original strict practice of St. Benedict. The first Cistercians saw themselves not as revolutionaries, but as reformers.

The Cistercian Order fell into the same pitfall as the Benedictines had before; as they became more successful and attracted more novices, the Cistercians became more prosperous and adopted looser rules. It fell to another Frenchman, Armand-Jean le Bouthillier de Rancé, to reform the order in the seventeenth century. He founded a new abbey at La Trappe (from which the name "Trappists" comes). Rancé and his followers became known as Cistercians of the Strict Observance, to distinguish them from their more relaxed colleagues. Merton later described Rancé's attitudes:

> The monks of La Trappe were encouraged to consider themselves as outcasts, rejected by God and men, and to find solace not in contemplation of God's love or of His mercy but only in the grim business of exercising justice upon their own bodies and souls by every kind of austerity and humiliation.
>
> That was why De Rancé placed such tremendous emphasis on the systematic tongue-lashings which he gave his monks in chapter and for which la Trappe soon became notorious. Monks were supposed to treasure above everything else these opportunities to accept "stinging reproaches, words of fire, public humiliation, and everything that could possibly contribute to their abasement."[29]

Remarkably, this harsh way of life encouraged more converts. The Trappist abbey was followed by a number of others. The

Trappist monasteries began largely as a French invention, but they soon attracted converts from other nations, especially Germany and Ireland. How, though, did the Order of the Strict Observance come to the United States?

The French Revolution, which started in 1789, was the catalyst. The revolution began as a moderate movement, but it turned radical by 1793, the year in which all monks and priests were obliged to swear loyalty to the new revolutionary government. Many priests and monks succumbed, but many others did not, and there was a fierce civil war in the area known as the Vendée, in west-central France. The Trappists could not abide the idea of swearing allegiance to a government rather than to God, and they made plans to emigrate. The United States, which had become popular among many Frenchmen because of the activities of the Marquis de Lafayette and others, seemed like a logical place to go.

There were many mishaps in the process. Some Trappists wound up in England and stayed there. The first handful crossed the Atlantic around the turn of the nineteenth century. They landed in Baltimore, but soon made their way to the forests of Kentucky, where they established the first Trappist lodging in the New World. A couple of years later, they moved on to Missouri. They settled on the left bank of the Mississippi River, a few miles downriver from the town of St. Louis (today it is East St. Louis).

Though they remained only about two years, the Trappist monks at St. Louis made a permanent entry into American history and folklore. Soon after they settled on the alluvial plains east of the Mississippi, they found that the landscape was exceptionally hilly and uneven. On further investiga-tion, they saw that the area was full of man-made mounds and hills. Their findings were not corroborated for some time, but when they were, Americans became aware that the Native Americans of the heartland had once built a great city just where the Trappists settled: Today it is Cahokia State Park, Illinois. The largest of the earthen hills was named "Monks' Mound" in honor of the Trappist monks who first discovered it.

This early settlement of Trappists did not endure. The monks went back to France, and the United States had to wait thirty years for the next wave of Cistercians to cross the Atlantic. A large group sailed from France in 1848 (which was another year of revolutions) and arrived in New Orleans. They took a steamboat upriver to Louisville, Kentucky, and founded the new Priory of Gethsemani on December 21, 1848 (it was elevated to an abbey in 1851).

The irony presented by this new abbey was not lost upon the people of the time. Here in America, where nearly everyone wanted to own land, sire a family, and grow rich, there were a number of Cistercian monks sworn to avoid all these things, and to seek instead stability, conversion of manners, and obedience. This made for a powerful contrast.

Americans indeed did not flock to join the abbey. Most of the recruits came from Europe, primarily from France, Ireland, and Germany. The handful of native Americans (people born on the continent, not necessarily American Indians) who joined the abbey all failed in their vocations: None of them was able to endure the rugged demands made by the order.

The lifestyle of a monk at Gethsemani, as later described by Merton, was as follows:

1. Rise at 2:00 A.M.
2. Go to choir.
3. Meditation at 2:30.
4. Communion at 4:00.
5. Breakfast at about 6:15.
6. Reading, study, or private prayer from 6:30 until 7:45.
7. High Mass at 7:45.[30]

The monks' day included two work sessions, one in the morning and another in the afternoon. It is no wonder that everyone was scheduled to be in bed by 7:00 P.M. The monks at Gethsemani probably endured a more demanding life than any other

Americans of the time—and this was the age of frontiersmen and cowboys!

Because virtually all of the American novices dropped out, much importance has been given to the first successful American at Gethsemani: His name was John Green Hanning, and pilgrims to Gethsemani today still ask to see his grave.[31]

Hanning came to Gethsemani in early middle age. He had grown up near Owensboro, Kentucky, and had known about the abbey since his youth, but he came to it in a very circuitous way. Hanning went out west and spent some years as a cowboy on the range. By the time he came to Gethsemani and took the name Brother Joachim, he had many qualities that seemed to argue against his becoming a monk, but also

THE COWBOY MONK

John Green Hanning was the son of Irish Catholic immigrants. He grew up near the Abbey of Gethsemani and had some schooling there. He quarreled with his father and at about the age of twenty went to Texas, where he spent ten years as a cowboy. From his youth, Hanning was known as a taciturn and unforgiving person: His favorite expression was, "I'll get even!"

Hanning returned home at about age thirty, and was engaged to be married when he felt a call to the abbey. He entered it in 1885 and became the first American to succeed at his vocation. After he became "Brother Joachim," Hanning became even more quiet, but his silence was now seen as evidence of his godliness. His temper and spirit remained a problem for many years, but he eventually learned to sublimate his spirit in the service of the abbey.

A wonderful photograph of Brother Joachim has an inscription on the back: "My sister, Mrs. Field, got one of the school boys to take Brother Joachim's picture. He ran away and when they caught him he closed his eyes."

By the time of his death in 1908, Brother Joachim had become an almost ideal monk. He defied the belief of the day that Americans could not make good monks, that they were too ill disciplined to "make it" in the monastery.

some others that made monastic life seem possible. According to Merton:

> Brother Joachim had many natural qualities that fitted him to be a Trappist brother. He was strong. He could work. And although for a good part of his life he had not lived as a Catholic, there was a predisposition to solitude, a natural foundation for the contemplative life, something he had acquired in those long, lonely rides on the range. But above all, he was sincere and already had much of the natural humility of men who have been too often beaten down by a dominant passion—of men who know their own weakness.[32]

Gethsemani came under the leadership of its first American abbot in 1935. Dom Frederic Dunne was still the abbot when Merton arrived six years later.

5

The Novice

*The ingenuous good humor that welled up
from time to time in the middle of all this made
their faces shine like the faces of children.*

—Thomas Merton, *The Seven Storey Mountain*

Merton was officially accepted as a postulant on St. Lucy's Day, December 13, 1941, and clothed as a novice on February 21, 1942, receiving the name "Louis." The world was now behind him. He could only move forward in this new life he had chosen.

The monastic life Merton entered in December 1941 was almost unbelievable to Americans of the time, and seems even more unbelievable to Americans of the twenty-first century. Trappist monks did not speak to one another except under extraordinary circumstances; instead, they used hand gestures and signs that had been developed by the order. The monks, of whom there were about one hundred thirty, lived in extremely close quarters; there was almost no privacy in the monastery. Monks could not leave the monastery walls; they were expected to live and die within the confines of the abbey.

There were even further restrictions. Monks could not take baths, and had to ask permission to take a shower. Clothing was distributed twice a year, and the monks were expected to make do and wear out all they possessed. Shoes could be repaired, it was true, but there was no remedy for the hot wool clothing, which gave nearly all the monks heat rash during the long summers. In spite of the discomfort engendered by heat, it was usually the cold that was most remembered; windows were left open much of the time, and the large wood stoves did little to heat the monks' one large dormitory. All in all, life at Our Lady of Gethsemani was probably as extreme as anything that could be experienced by an American in the twentieth century.

There was a part of Merton that delighted in the hardships. He had never been one to seek much in the way of worldly comfort, and neither the heat nor the cold caused him much distress. He was very hardy in his twenties and thirties, but in his forties, he would experience numerous health problems, some of them systemic and some of them caused by the rigors of the monastic lifestyle. But what one wonders most is: How did the man of a thousand—indeed, a million—words, handle the experience of not being able to speak?

Merton had no complaints at first. He seems to have delighted in the first order and discipline of his adult life. Ever since the death of his mother, he had been involved in the world, but was something of a stranger to it: He had lived in apartments, traveled on trains, but had never felt at home in any place. Now, at Gethsemani, he experienced the first real home he had ever known. He described some of his early impressions of monastic life:

> The imperfections are much smaller and more trivial than the defects and vices of people outside in the world: and yet somehow you tend to notice them more and feel them more, because they get to be so greatly magnified by the responsibilities and ideals of the religious state, through which you cannot help looking at them. . . .
>
> With the novices, their sensible piety was innocent and spontaneous, and it was perfectly proper to their state. As a matter of fact I liked the novitiate at once. It was pervaded with enthusiasm and vitality and good humor.
>
> I liked the way they kidded one another in sign language, and I liked the quiet storms of amusement that suddenly blew up from . . . time to time. Practically all the novices seemed to be very enlightened and sincere about their duties in the religious life; they had been quick in catching on to the rules and were keeping them with spontaneous ease rather than hair-splitting exactitude. And the ingenuous good humor that welled up from time to time in the middle of all this made their faces shine like the faces of children—even though some of them were no longer young.[33]

Who were these monks who were no longer young? They tended to be, on average, about the age of thirty. Gethsemani had long had a tradition of recruiting its novices from Europe, but by the time Merton arrived in 1941, Americans were in the ascendant. In the five years that followed, Gethsemani received quite a few other novices, many of them veterans of World War II who wanted to escape from the horrors of the outside world.

Today, in the early twenty-first century, someone at Merton's age of twenty-six is still considered young. This was not the case in the 1940s. With the exception of a small minority of Americans who had trust funds, most people were expected to find a vocation (whether that meant work, marriage, family, or all of these) by about the age of twenty-five. Anyone over twenty-five and certainly anyone over the age of thirty who did not have a definite station in life was looked upon with suspicion. The youth revolution that would occur in the 1960s would be a result of the "Baby Boom" that took place after 1945. But the world of 1941, and especially the monastic world Merton had entered, demanded conformity and certainty from its members. After all, there was "a war on"—against Hitler and Nazism.

The war came back to Merton through the appearance of his younger brother, John Paul. He had been accepted into the Royal Canadian Air Force, and came down to Gethsemani to bid farewell to Merton. Rather surprisingly, John Paul expressed a desire to be accepted into the Catholic Church. Merton undertook to educate his younger brother over a period of seven days, after which John Paul was baptized. He left a few days later, and the older brother watched the younger one depart:

> I went to see him off at the Gate. . . . A visitor gave him a ride to Bardstown. As the car was turning around to start down the avenue, John Paul turned around and waved, and it was only then that his expression showed some possibility that he might be realizing, as I did, that we would never see each other on earth again.[34]

John Paul was killed in a bombing mission to Mannheim, Germany, the following April. Merton, who had found a new set of "brothers" at the monastery, had to grieve the loss of his one blood brother, who was the last of his immediate kin.

For all the wandering in which he had previously engaged, Merton was fundamentally an anxious, driven soul. Therefore, it meant a great deal to him to have the matter of his vocation settled; he was probably happier in his first months at the monastery than he had been at any time since the death of his father in 1931.

As months passed, Merton became aware of the rigidity presupposed by the life he had chosen. He learned that he could not send letters except on four occasions during the year. He also found each person was allowed only one hour a day to let his thoughts roam or to rest; even sleep was closely regulated (monks slept on what were essentially benches, wearing long underwear that chafed the skin). We cannot keep track of any "complaints" Merton may have had, for he did not resume his journal writing until 1946. But almost from the start of his time at Gethsemani, Merton was indeed engaged in writing; he was editing, chopping away parts of essays he had written in the past, and he was gathering up material to send to his literary agent, Naomi Burton. The wanderer had become a monk, but his mind and his pen wandered still. Later, Merton would write:

> In the silence of the countryside and the forest, in the cloistered solitude of my monastery, I have discovered the whole Western Hemisphere. Here I have been able, through the grace of God, to explore the New World, without traveling from city to city, without flying over the Andes or the Amazon, stopping one day here, two there, and then continuing on. Perhaps If I had traveled in this manner, I should have seen nothing: generally those who travel the most see the least.[35]

This new belief in the efficacy of the travel of the mind would sustain Merton for many years. It is important to remember that he and his fellow monks received almost no news of or from the outside world. Merton did not know about the great European battles of World War II, or the desperate fights between Americans and Japanese in the Pacific. He and his fellow monks did learn that the atomic bomb had been dropped, but they did not know that it was President Harry Truman, rather than the late President Franklin D. Roosevelt, who had commissioned its use.

After two years of rather intense discipline and training, Merton's fragile health began to give way. He was transferred to the task of research on the history of the Cistercian Order, and he also worked on his autobiography, outlining how he came to be a monk. The first work culminated in *The Waters of Siloe*, published in 1949, and the second finished with *The Seven Storey Mountain*, published by Harcourt Brace late in 1948. Seldom has a book been received in the manner of *The Seven Storey Mountain.*

Robert Giroux at Harcourt Brace scheduled an initial press run of 20,000 copies, which for most books of its genre would be a modest success. Harcourt Brace was soon printing the book by the tens of thousands. All this was accomplished without much in the way of publicity; *The Seven Storey Mountain* either sold itself or was purchased because of word of mouth. The great question was, and remains: What drew so many people to buy and read *The Seven Storey Mountain*? There are many possible answers. The two that come to mind when viewed over the distance of fifty-five years are: prose and timing.

Merton was already a master of prose. He had been writing since he was five, and his hunger for words had never decreased. Nor were his words all sweet. He understood a good deal of the social and racial divides that existed in the United States. For example, he wrote about Harlem:

> Harlem is, in a sense, what God thinks of Hollywood. And Hollywood is all Harlem has, in its despair, to grasp at, by way of a surrogate for heaven.
>
> The most terrible thing about it all is that there is not a Negro in the whole place who does not realize, somewhere in the depths of his nature, that the culture of the white

men is not worth the dirt in Harlem's gutters. They sense
that the whole thing is rotten, that it is a fake, that it is spu-
rious, empty, a shadow of nothingness. And yet they are
condemned to reach out for it, and to seem to desire it, and
to pretend they like it, as if the whole thing were some kind
of bitter cosmic conspiracy: as if they were thus being
forced to work out, in their own lives, a clear representation
of the misery which has corrupted the ontological roots of
the white man's own existence.[36]

These were powerful words for someone who had been locked
away from the world for the past seven years!

Merton also had strong feelings about the U.S. entry into World
War II, which he had just missed by entering the monastery.
Writing as if he were back in mid-1941, he mused:

For a war to be just, it must be a war of defence. A war of
aggression is not just. If America entered the war now,
would it be a war of aggression? I suppose if you wanted to
get subtle about it, you could work out some kind of an
argument to that effect. But I personally could not see that
it would be anything else than legitimate self-defense. How
legitimate? To answer that, I would have had to be a moral
theologian and a diplomat and a historian and a politician
and probably also a mind-reader.[37]

The second reason for Merton's popularity is one of timing.
Americans in 1948 were eager for something other than the
six o'clock evening news over the radio. They were weary of
hearing about Berlin and the new war against communism.
Millions of young American men had served in World War II,
and, instead of being rewarded with peace, they were expected
to be vigilant against the new enemy represented by the Soviet
Union. Merton had some choice words about that as well. He
recalled his own brief flirtation with communism during his
student days:

I don't think even I was gullible enough to swallow all the business about the ultimate bliss that would follow the withering away of the state—a legend far more naïve and far more oversimplified than the happy hunting ground of the most primitive Indian. . . .

The chief weakness of Communism is that it is, itself, only another breed of the same materialism which is the source and root of all the evils which it so clearly sees, and it is evidently nothing but another product of the break-down of the capitalist system. Indeed, it seems to be pieced together out of the ruins of the same ideology that once went into the vast, amorphous, intellectual structure underlying capitalism in the nineteenth century.[38]

The proof, as they say, is in the pudding. Merton's pudding was *The Seven Storey Mountain,* and the people who tasted it generally thought it was the grandest thing written in their time. Review after rave review poured into newspapers around the country. All around the country, readers had discovered a new type of literary hero, and he was Thomas Merton rather than Ernest Hemingway. Merton had done something no previous American writer had done: opened the general reading public to a view of mysticism and solitude that was distinctly *American,* despite Merton's own ancestral roots in France.

Since the first publication of *The Seven Storey Mountain,* Merton has become just about the most-read American mystic of any time period. The great American theologian Jonathan Edwards (1703–1758) had published many great works, but they were seldom read by the general public. Merton, on the other hand, had brought mysticism to the American public.

6

Priest and Rebel

You want a hermitage in Times Square
with a large sign over it saying HERMIT.

—Dr. Gregory Zilboorg to Merton in 1956

Merton was ordained a priest on May 26, 1949. Several of his good friends from his Columbia days came south to be with him at this moment. Even on the very morning of his ordination, Merton was listed in the Chapter of Faults: The offense was that his friends had blocked doorways while photographs were taken of them. Merton struggled with all his conflicted feelings about Gethsemani and the life of a monk, but his friends were not aware of this conflict. He chatted joyfully with them, and was astonished to learn that Harry Truman had become president, and that the Communists were close to a complete takeover of China. Three days after the event, Merton wrote in his journal:

> I wish I could explain something about the gradation that seems to have marked the three days of my festival. Each one seemed to represent some gigantic development that I am powerless to grasp or explain. In the end I had the impression that all who came to see me were dispersing to the four corners of the universe with hymns and messages and prophecies, speaking with tongues and ready to raise the dead because the fact is for three days we have been full of the Holy Ghost and the Spirit of God seemed to be taking greater and greater possession of all our souls through the first three Masses of my life, my three greatest graces. . . .
>
> It seems like the triumphant conclusion of an epoch and the beginning of a new history whose implications are utterly beyond me.[39]

Just three days later, Merton was part of the festivities to celebrate the hundredth anniversary of the Abbey of Gethsemani. Merton and others felt that the celebration itself was in some small way a betrayal of the goals of silence and solitude. Archbishop Fulton Sheen appeared and spoke loudly over a microphone, and the day's events did not truly honor the spirit in which Gethsemani had been born. But all was over in twenty-four hours, and Merton and his community returned to their daily routines.

Dom James had now been the abbot of Gethsemani for about two years. Dom James and Merton were two very different souls, but each man's life purpose nevertheless required the service of the other. Dom James was much more pragmatic and business-like than Merton was, but the monks testified that he was capable of extraordinary personal warmth. Much of Merton's struggle over the next few years would be with Dom James. Could the monk, now a priest, ask for and receive permission to find greater solitude, in whatever small way? Would the monk and priest who had now become an abbot consent?

Dom James made Merton master of scholastics in 1951, then in 1955, master of novices. This was exciting work, but also highly demanding. Gethsemani was booming that year, and in the mid-1950s, Merton had no less than forty young novices to instruct. One of the best views of Merton as a teacher comes from Flavian Burns, who entered the monastery in 1951.

Burns had read *The Seven Storey Mountain* a few years earlier, and had been greatly taken by the book's message, but he was not impressed at first with Merton as a person. Burns came to Gethsemani intending to find his own way spiritually and not to fall into the increasing crowd of Merton devotees. But, as he described it, Merton's teaching had an infectious quality that was difficult to resist, and Burns, too, became a Merton admirer:

> I liked him enormously in the scholasticate—everyone did—because, while he could be serious in his spiritual direction talks, he was full of humor and jokes, and always buoyant.
>
> Like the first time I recognized him in the monastery; it was after the bell had rung and all two hundred monks were filing through the cloisters to the church. And there, coming down the middle of the cloister in the opposite direction, was this one man, making signs to everybody, explaining why he was going in the wrong direction. And then he would tease us in class about not believing in silence. He would

say, "Why, you fellows can't even pass one another in the corridor without making some silly sign," which of course he did himself. He was a master at visual commentary, like during the readings in the refectory or during the chapter talks. Just with the raise of his eyebrows or a facial expression of horror at what was being said or proposed, he could bring down the house in laughter.[40]

Apparently, the students had more fun under Merton's direction than had been the case in the past. But if Merton let himself go in levity, he must also have been an excellent teacher, for Dom James would never have allowed anything else in the scholasticate.

By the mid-1950s, Merton was showing unmistakable signs of strain. His health was unsteady; he often suffered from problems with his teeth. This can be attributed to the diet of the monks at Gethsemani, which was extremely limited— sauerkraut and potatoes were eaten at virtually every meal— but some of his physical troubles stemmed from earlier times: His "scare" on the Long Island Rail Road had been the early signs of gastritis. He had been furiously productive for the past twelve years, writing as many as fifteen books, as well as becoming a priest and teaching the students. The wonder is not that he showed the signs, but rather that they had been put off for as long as they were.

The single greatest issue between Merton and Dom James was that of "stability," which in monastic terms means the ability to remain stable in one monastery: to fully commit to that place. Merton had long flirted with other ideas. All of them he dressed up in ways to make them more palatable to his superiors. He claimed he wanted to join the Carthusians (another order of monks), who had a new monastery in Vermont. He wanted to play a role in forming new Cistercian monasteries. But these all added up to the same root motivation: Merton wanted to leave Gethsemani in search of greater solitude. As Merton biographer Michael Mott has explained it:

The main contention between James Fox and Thomas Merton was over trust. . . . Dom James trusted Father Louis within the monastery and he showed that trust. He did not trust Merton outside the enclosure walls. In time the abbot showed trust in others. He made his lack of confidence in Father Louis all too obvious to Merton, and nothing rankled Merton more than this.[41]

DOM JAMES (FOX)

James Fox was born and brought up in the Boston area. He was among the first generation of Boston Irish to "make it" financially; he went to Harvard University, and graduated from its business school at the age of twenty-one. By the time he joined the Cistercians, Fox had already proven himself to be a man of intelligence, resolution, and considerable personal warmth.

Fox had been at Gethsemani before Merton arrived in 1941. When Fox came back to the abbey in 1948 as the new abbot, Merton and others knew at once that this would not be "business as usual." Dom James kept an immaculate office; he held to a demanding schedule, and insisted upon the same type of perfection from his monks. His favorite saying, a Cistercian one, was: "All for Jesus, through Mary, with a smile."

Quite possibly it was that smile that enraged Thomas Merton so much over the years. Dom James enjoyed being the figure of authority, even relished it, and Merton was a born questioner, even a rebel. Despite their differences, though, Merton and Dom James recognized the greatness within one another. Merton would later claim that he "needed" Dom James to keep him honest.

Their relationship began well, but foundered for a time. There was bitterness on both sides as the years went by. The two seemed close to making up when Dom James announced his retirement in 1967. He retired to a hermitage of his own, on the abbey grounds.

The struggles between Dom James and Merton were sometimes personal, but there was always a transcendent theme as well. One man believed implicitly in authority and continuity, while the other admired risk-taking and change.

It is easy to sympathize with Merton. One naturally feels for a man of such wide-ranging talents who was cooped up in one place for so long. But it does not take much of a stretch to sympathize with Dom James. He had, in Merton, something of a gold mine. Merton's books brought money to Gethsemani and they also brought new postulants. If Merton left, so would these by-products, and worse yet, Gethsemani would be known as the place that Merton had chosen and then abandoned. So the legacy of *The Seven Storey Mountain* was not just one of success: It also helped entrap Merton at Gethsemani.

The abbey had boomed during the past five years. Many novices were accepted into the ranks, and the place became ever more crowded. Many of the reasons for entry were the same as before—the desire to leave an unfriendly world—but some of the new monks were devotees of Merton; they had read *The Seven Storey Mountain* and it had changed their lives. Because of this influence, Merton made a point of never discussing his own writing in his classes for the novices; they did not even know that some of the evening meditations, read aloud, came from his pen.

Merton was increasingly pained by the lack of privacy— which he always called "solitude"—at the abbey. The monks lived a life of relentless togetherness, but were expected not to make conversation or form close friendships. How unnatural this was for someone with Merton's temperament!

A visit from the outside revealed both the positive and negative aspects of Merton's life. In the spring of 1956, Mark Van Doren and his wife made a trip to Kentucky. They visited Merton at Gethsemani, and Van Doren later wrote to explain his feelings at that moment:

> When Merton came, grinning, to shake our hands and make
> us welcome, I was stupid enough to be startled because he
> had altered in no respect from the mirthful student I once
> knew. Thirteen years had passed, and of course he looked a

little older; but as we sat and talked I could see no important difference in him, and once I interrupted a reminiscence of his by laughing. "Tom," I said, "you haven't changed at all." "Why should I? Here," he said, "our duty is to be more ourselves, not less." It was a searching remark and I stood happily corrected. . . .

My final thought as I looked back and waved was about how wrong anyone would be who considered him a prisoner in that place. He seemed a happy man if I ever saw one: serene and certain, grave and smiling, utterly serious and utterly free.[42]

Yet even Mark Van Doren could be mistaken. Merton was, in fact, near despair. He was frantically busy, working to meet the needs of the forty students in the novitiate. He was in charge of taking care of the abbey's forests, and he was also trying to fit in time to write. Seldom has any person in the contemplative life attempted to do so much at once.

Busy-ness, which Merton often referred to as the curse of the world, had caught up with him. Increasingly tired and strained, he needed some friendship to make up for what he could not obtain through solitude.

Merton was making new friends in the monastery. One of them was John Eudes Bamberger, a medical doctor who entered the monastery in 1950. Bamberger later described his first impressions of Merton as a teacher:

And then one day we had a lecture by Father Louis, as we called Merton there, but I never would have picked him out to be the one. He was a very different type than the image he projected in his writings. He was a very outgoing person with an obvious ease with relationships, very approachable, with a great sense of humor.[43]

Merton and Bamberger began to work together in a type of system to "screen" the incoming novices. Bamberger was an obvious choice, because of his medical training, and he and Merton went to work determining if applicants had both the right attitude and the personal strength needed to "make it" at the abbey.

In the course of their work together, Merton sometimes admitted to Bamberger that he felt inadequate in the use of psychological and medical technology. Typically, Merton threw himself into a short study of the subject, and before long, he had written an essay entitled "Neurosis in the Monastic Life." Merton sent the essay to his publisher, who asked if he had any objections to the essay being read by another author with the same firm: the renowned psychiatrist Gregory Zilboorg. Merton said he would be pleased to have Zilboorg read the essay.

Merton did not know that Zilboorg had already done what he considered an analysis of Merton, conducted from his writings. Zilboorg was convinced that Merton was on the verge of a serious breakdown, and that any writing Merton might do on the subject of psychology would only worsen the situation. So when Merton went on his first major trip outside the abbey—to a conference at St. John's University in Minnesota in 1956—he had no idea that he had been "set up" for analysis by Zilboorg. One of the most painful scenes of Merton's life ensued.

On the third day of the conference, Zilboorg managed to speak with Merton alone. Merton later recorded much of what happened, along with many of Zilboorg's words, in his journal:

> It turns out *he* [Zilboorg] was the one who engineered my coming here. . . .
>
> It turns out also—as I know—that I am in somewhat bad shape, and that I *am* neurotic. . . .
>
> "You are a gadfly to your superiors."
>
> "Very stubborn—You keep coming back until you get what you want."
>
> "You are afraid to be an ordinary monk in the community."[44]

At another time and place, Merton might have freely admitted to most of these charges. He knew that he had the heart and spirit of a rebel: That may be why he chose the monastic life, as a way of keeping his natural impulses in check. Merton did conjecture, in his journal, that he was more like his grandfather, Pop, than he had previously thought. It had been Pop who told him, "Don't think, follow hunches." So Merton may have been able to accept this critique of his character if it came from someone he knew and respected. But Merton did not know Zilboorg, and this "analysis" seemed like a personal attack. Shaken by the experience, Merton stayed away from Zilboorg until later in the conference, when Zilboorg brought Dom James and Merton together for what the psychiatrist believed would be a frank and earnest talk.

Merton was appalled at being exposed in front of the abbot, his superior in the monastery's hierarchy. Merton burst into tears and screamed in rage, something he had done very infrequently in his life. Despite his restless temperament, Merton usually kept a cheerful look about him. Perhaps the greatest humiliation came when the doctor accused Merton of wanting fame: "You want a hermitage in Times Square with a large sign over it saying 'HERMIT.' "[45] This was probably the worst day in Merton's life since he had entered the abbey in 1941.

The crisis subsided, and both Merton and Dom James returned to Gethsemani. The two tried to pick up where they had left off, but Merton nursed a quiet bitterness toward Dom James, believing that he was responsible for summoning the psychiatrist and bringing about the public humiliation. Relations improved slowly, but Merton remained wary of the abbot for some time to come.

As the 1950s wound down, Merton was still viewed with some concern at the monastery. He had survived the greatest test to his monastic "stability," but he was now beginning to agitate for a hermitage, a place where he could spend a few hours of each day by himself.

Meanwhile, changes were taking place in the Roman Catholic Church. A new pope, John XXIII, had been elected, and he seemed determined to bring about some much-needed reforms. Merton and the other monks at Gethsemani eagerly awaited the start of a new decade, one that would indeed bring many changes.

7

The Second Vatican Council

It is all part of the same sickness,
it all hangs together.

—Merton's Journals

Merton and many other Catholics were dismayed by the Church's position in the world. Roman Catholicism seemed to be out of touch with the twentieth century. Then came a new pope and a new approach to Roman Catholicism.

Angelo Giuseppe Roncalli became Pope John XXIII late in 1958. Within a year of becoming the pontiff, he announced that a major council would be held in Rome in 1962. Eventually, some 2,500 bishops from all around the world accepted the invitation. The Second Vatican Council convened on October 12, 1962.

Although he did not attend, Merton commented on the Vatican Council in his journal:

> The opening was great. John's opening speech was that of a very great, charismatic Pope. Also he received the diplomats in the Sistine Chapel, pointed up to Michelangelo's Last Judgment and said: "Well gentlemen, what will it be?"
>
> He said what needed to be said, and said it forcefully and directly. He said the people of the world want peace. That God will severely judge the rulers who fail in their responsibility to their people.[46]

Merton knew few of the details of what was happening in Rome, and even less about what was happening in the Cuban Missile Crisis—the dangerous standoff between the United States, Cuba, and the Soviet Union.

Early in 1962, American spy planes detected the presence of Soviet-made missiles in Cuba. Since it came to power, the Kennedy administration had been quietly at war with the Communist Cuban government of Fidel Castro, attempting to bring down what was the only Communist regime in the Western Hemisphere. The Soviet Union had responded by sending missiles, ostensibly to protect Cuba, but American policymakers believed those weapons were, in fact, aimed at the United States.

President John Kennedy went on television in mid-October.

He cautioned the American public that they were in a time of great danger, and he warned the Soviet government to back off in its support for Castro's Cuba. In the same week that Pope John welcomed the cardinals and bishops to Rome, the world witnessed the gravest confrontation yet seen between the two nuclear superpowers.

Days passed and the tension grew. The Soviet delegates to the United Nations continued to insist that any weapons they had in Cuba were purely defensive; the Americans delegates insisted that the missiles were offensive weapons directed at the United States. President Kennedy had the U.S. Navy blockade the island of Cuba. As Soviet ships approached, the world came close to a

THE FIRST CATHOLIC PRESIDENT

Gethsemani was one of the least "political" places in all of North America, but the presidential candidacy of John Kennedy, a Roman Catholic, made even the monks and novices pay more attention to politics, at least for the year 1960.

Catholicism was perceived to be almost a kiss of death in American politics. The only Roman Catholic even to have run for president was Alfred Smith, who was soundly defeated by Herbert Hoover in the 1928 election. Therefore, it was a major event when John Kennedy of Massachusetts announced his candidacy in 1960.

Kennedy was certainly a rather secular Catholic. He and his brothers had been raised on the ethics of competition and success, rather than cooperation and humility. But there were still many commentators who believed that Kennedy would be undone by his Catholicism—that the nation would not accept a Roman Catholic who might be persuaded to take orders from the pope.

Kennedy confronted this charge head-on. He met with a number of Protestant bishops in Houston, Texas, where he assured them that religion and politics were separate in his mind and heart. From that moment on, his Catholicism was much less of a factor in the campaign.

Kennedy won the 1960 election by the narrowest of margins. But once he took office in January 1961 his charm and wit began to work their magic; within the space of a year, he had become one of the most admired men of his time.

nuclear confrontation. Then, the Soviets backed down. The Soviet ships headed for Cuba turned away, rather than confront the blockading American vessels.

The world was saved, for the moment. President Kennedy became a great hero in the United States, and American power was praised around the globe. But few Americans knew at the time how very close the Soviets had come to calling Kennedy's bluff, and later histories would indicate that Kennedy—egged on by his younger brother, Attorney General Robert Kennedy—had risked nuclear war.

What did Merton know or think about these developments? He was less sheltered now, and news came more readily to Gethsemani than it had in the past. But his journal indicates that now he was wrestling both with his inner demons and with the threats of war. Just about one year before the Cuban Missile Crisis, in October 1961, Merton confided to his journal:

> Letter from Jim Forest at the *Catholic Worker*—that my article on the "War Madness" is published and that there will be controversy about it. That everyone has gone crazy, building fallout shelters and preparing to shoot their neighbors. Whole towns preparing to defend themselves against neighboring towns. What do the Russians need with bombs at all? Just get a false alarm going and we will all shoot each other up without giving them further trouble! A nice testimony to democracy and individualism![47]

Merton had long since despaired both of American individualism and Soviet totalitarianism. He had briefly flirted with communism during his student days at Columbia University, but had soon come to the conclusion that no governmental system, no engine designed by human beings, could really save the world. Only an effort to reach God and to act in a more Christian way could save the planet from destruction.

Soon he had another concern. On December 11, 1962, Merton

noted the arrival of a review of a new work by Rachel Carson. Carson's book, *Silent Spring*, has been hailed ever since as one of the landmark publications of the environmental movement; in it, she pointed out what the indiscriminate use of pesticides was doing to the bird population of the United States. Her prophecy has long since been vindicated. Americans who were alive in the 1930s and 1940s claim that the noise of birds on spring and summer mornings was deafening, and that one could not sleep past five in the morning in rural areas. Today we live in a landscape with a much diminished bird population. Merton confided to his journal:

> Someone will say: you worry about birds. Why not worry about people? I worry about *both* birds and people. We are in the world and part of it, and we are destroying every-thing because we are destroying ourselves spiritually, morally, and in every way. It is all part of the same sickness, it all hangs together.[48]

Merton was becoming more socially conscious. Sometimes it chafed him to be in the monastery where only his words could reach the outside world. As 1962 gave way to 1963, he took stock of his situation. He wrote an especially candid journal entry on May 26, 1963:

> Today is the fourteenth anniversary of my Ordination to the priesthood.
>
> I wish I could say that they had been fourteen years of ever-growing fulfillment and order and integration. That is unfortunately not so. They have been years of relative happiness and productivity on the surface, but now I real-ize more and more the depth of my frustration and the apparent finality of my defeat. I have certainly not fitted into the conventional—or even traditional—mold. . . . I have a very real sense that it [my monastic life] has all been some kind of a lie, a charade. With all my blundering

attempts at sincerity, I have actually done nothing to change this. . . .

Probably the chief weakness has been lack of real courage to bear up under the attention of monastic and priestly life. Anyway, I am worn down. I am easily discouraged. The depressions are deeper, more frequent. I am near fifty. People think I am happy.[49]

Pope John XXIII died about one week later. Merton mourned the passing of this great and good man who had done so much to reinvigorate the Church. The new pope, Paul VI, announced that the Second Vatican Council would continue.

A second great loss came in November of the same year, when President John Kennedy was assassinated in Dallas. Like millions of other Americans, Merton could hardly believe the news. Americans from all backgrounds had become deeply attached to the handsome, tanned, and youthful president.

In a sense, the middle part of Merton's life as a monk ended around this time in 1963. If he remained hearty, and if he continued to write, he yearned for something less confining than the monastic life, and he was about to receive it.

Between 1961 and 1963, Merton was hard at work on his *Conjectures of a Guilty Bystander*. Though the book was published in 1966, it is much more revealing of Merton's thought during the Vatican Council and the Cuban Missile Crisis than it is of, say, 1965 and 1966, when he was absorbed by news of the Vietnam War. The following selections from *Conjectures* give a portrait of what Merton's mental landscape was between 1961 and 1963. He wrote: "Karl Barth had a dream about Mozart."[50] Mozart, of course, needs no introduction. Karl Barth was the world's most prominent Protestant theologian. Born in Switzerland in 1886, he had spent most of his life as a pastor or a university professor, first in Germany and then in Switzerland. Merton goes on:

Each day, for years, Barth played Mozart every morning before going to work on his dogma: unconsciously seeking to awaken, perhaps, the hidden sophianic Mozart in himself, the central wisdom that comes in tune with the divine and cosmic music and is saved by love, yes, even by *eros*. While the other, theological self, seemingly more concerned with love, grasps at a more stern, more cerebral *agape*: a love that, after all, is not in our own heart but *only in God* and revealed only to our head.[51]

Merton referred to the ancient terms of *eros* and *agape*. The former refers to romantic love; the latter refers to a Christ-like type of dispassionate love. Merton was certainly not the first Catholic writer to accuse a leading Protestant of favoring agape over eros, but Merton had struggled with these conflicting feelings for many years. Merton had a message for Karl Barth: "Fear not, Karl Barth! Trust in the divine mercy. Though you have grown up to become a theologian, Christ remains a child in you. Your books (and mine) matter less than we might think! There is in us a Mozart who will be our salvation."[52]

Conjectures of a Guilty Bystander was definitely a departure for Merton. Even though *The Seven Storey Mountain* might be termed a work of "stream of consciousness," it held together much more coherently than *Conjectures*. The latter book, penned about fifteen years after *The Seven Storey Mountain*, shows a much more disparate Merton, one who likes his fellow monks one day, and who casts quiet criticism on them the next. He had some especially strong words for the United States and what might be called the American myth:

When a myth becomes an evasion, the society that clings to it gets into serious trouble.

What is the conventionally accepted American myth? Is this myth still alive, or has it expired and become an evasion? Is the present crisis—in race relations, delinquency, etc., a judgment of our public daydream?

"America is the earthly paradise."[53]

Merton explained, at some length, that Americans needed to realize that they were in the same boat as everyone else: that there was no special providence watching over the United States. Providence looks out for all nations to the same degree; there is no favoritism in the Kingdom of God. Having laid bare what he believed to be the failed American myth, Merton then delved into sociology, and described the failed lives of so many people in the civilized "First" World:

> A great deal of virtue and piety is simply the easy price we pay in order to justify a life that is essentially trifling. Nothing is so cheap as the evasion purchased by just enough good conduct to make one pass as a "serious person." . . .
>
> In our society, a society of business rooted in puritanism, based on a pseudo-ethic of industriousness and thrift, to be rewarded by comfort, pleasure, and a good bank account, the myth of work is thought to justify an existence that is essentially meaningless and futile. There is, then a great deal of busy-ness as people invent things to do when in fact there is very little to be done. Yet we are overwhelmed with jobs, duties, tasks, assignments, "missions" of every kind.[54]

These words were almost certainly a reflection of Merton's life at the time. Since 1955, he had been overstretched, tending to the novices, to the forests around Gethsemani, and to his writing. He once complained of the incredible irony that a person devoted to the contemplative life should be so constantly on the verge of a physical breakdown.

Merton went on to describe the current version of the American myth: "And today? All we do is watch ourselves in the mirror of TV. Yes, that is you and me, pardner. Tight-lipped, straight-shooting, hard-hitting, clean-loving: we are still on the frontier, we are still in paradise. There has really been no history."[55]

Something of a paradox exists here. Merton had been secluded from the world for over twenty years. How did he know what the television was showing in the mid-1960s?

Many people, when deprived of one the five senses, develop the other four more keenly. This can be said of Merton, in an analogy, to suggest how well he kept his hand on the pulse of everyday America. If he did not watch television or read many newspapers, he took every opportunity to speak with people and to learn about their daily lives. No matter how he learned about everyday life, Merton was pretty accurate in his depiction of it.

One of Merton's keenest insights came when he pondered how other nationalities around the world viewed the United States:

> It suddenly dawned on me that the anti-Americanism in the world today is a hatred as deep and as lasting and as all-inclusive as anti-Semitism. And just about as rational. I see now that I must understand myself in the light of this hatred. To identify myself completely with this country is like accepting the fact of a hidden Jewish grandfather in Nazi Germany. My European background gives me a protective coloring, no doubt. I am, as it were, a Jew with blond hair and blue eyes. But no, I remain a citizen of a hated nation, and no excuses will serve. I know for a fact that this does have some influence on the way my books are received in some places in Europe.[56]

Once again, we can marvel at how well Merton kept abreast of current events. He was even ahead of his time, for many Americans imagined they were beloved by other nations of the world in the 1960s. But Merton correctly perceived that American power—both military and economic—had earned the nation quiet enemies around the globe.

Merton was no longer the thirty-year-old monk who had written *The Seven Storey Mountain*. Sometimes, in his journals, he questioned whether he could ever write something so optimistic

THOMAS MERTON

Merton outside the new hermitage, just after it was built. This would be the first place of privacy he had experienced in over twenty years.

Merton (right) with his father, his grandmother, and his baby brother. Merton had already taken notice that his brother had an easier, more lovable nature than his own.

Merton's ordination took place in May 1949. He is seen at the lower right.

This photograph of Gethsemani does something to portray the stark life of the monks. The Order of Cistercians of the Strict Observance meant just that—no comforts.

Merton drew this sketch of the abbey. Some of his biographers point out that he was always drawn, from his earliest years, to medieval signs, shapes, and symbols.

Merton's "Tree of Life" seems almost to betray his pantheistic inclinations. He was happiest when in nature, and his faith was full of natural inspirations.

Merton in a rare moment of satisfaction. He and three of
the novices, whom he instructed, at the abbey. He was a
teacher and mentor of rare talent.

Merton with His Holiness, the Fourteenth Dalai Lama of Tibet. The two men found much common ground.

again, even concerning the contemplative life. Merton was aware of the complexities and the contradictions both within modern society and within himself.

Conjectures of a Guilty Bystander was published in 1966. By then, Merton had achieved one of his long deferred dreams: He had become a hermit.

8

The Hermit

*S. [or M, as Merton referred to her] was at last
the ideal reader—the Lara, perhaps, to his Yuri.*

—Michael Mott,
The Seven Mountains of Thomas Merton

Merton had long yearned for more privacy. In the mid-1950s, he had asked Dom James about the possibility of having a hermitage on the grounds of Gethsemani. The abbot had decided that Merton, who was already the abbey's forester, could also serve as its firewatcher. There was a fire tower on the abbey grounds. Dom James suggested that Merton live atop the tower and come to the abbey for one meal and one set of prayers a day. To the abbot's surprise, Merton turned him down at that point, claiming he did not wish to become another Simeon Stylites (a fifth-century hermit who lived on top of a pillar for many years).

Merton finally got his wish in 1965. He was allowed to resign as novice master and take up residence in a hermitage half a mile from the abbey. A crude cabin was built to the extent that Trappist rules allowed, and Merton moved in. Though this relocation may seem extremely limited to people living in the secular world, it was an enormous step for Merton, who finally attained some of the peace and relaxation he desperately needed.

He had given so much to the abbey and his fellow monks. He had practically raised a generation of novices, and now he wanted time to think, pause, and reflect. Of course, this was not the type of gentle, calm thinking that some would pursue, but the vigorous, even peripatetic, thinking of Thomas Merton. He appears to have kept abreast of many current books, since his journal entry shows he had read Marshall McLuhan's *Media and the Mind of Man*, published in 1964:

> The hermit life is cool. It is a life of low definition in which there is little to decide, in which there are few transactions or none, in which there are no packages to be delivered. In which I do not bundle up packages and deliver them to myself. It is not intense. There is no give and take of questions and answers, problems and solutions. Problems begin down the hill. Over there under the water tower are solutions. Here there are woods, foxes. Here there is no need for dark glasses. "Here" does not even warm itself up with references to "there." It is just a "here" for which there is no "there." The hermit life is that cool.[57]

Merton was using Marshall McLuhan's contrast between "cool" media, such as the telephone, and "hot" ones, such as the television. He went on: "The monastic life as a whole is a hot medium. Hot with words like *must, ought,* and *should.* Communities are devoted to high-definition projects: 'making it all clear!' The clearer it gets the clearer it has to be made. It branches out. You have to keep clearing the branches." [58]

In that same journal entry, Merton conducted a dialogue with himself:

> Why live in the woods?
>> Well, you have to live somewhere.
>
> Do you get lonely?
>> Yes, sometimes.
>
> Are you mad at people?
>> No.
>
> Are you mad at the monastery?
>> No.
>
> What do you think about the future of monasticism?
>> Nothing. I don't think about it.
>
> Is it true that your bad back is due to Yoga?
>> No.
>
> Is it true that you are practicing Zen in secret?
>> Pardon me, I don't speak English. [59]

Humor pops up as always in Merton's writing, but there is also a refreshing new sense of freedom. One gets the sense that Merton finally felt he had atoned for the sins of his youth, that his years of labor, both in the woods and in the novitiate, had compensated for his early transgressions. He seems ready to be free.

At the same time, physical troubles were catching up with him. Merton had always been a strange combination of hale and hearty, along with bouts of intense weakness and sickness. In

March 1966, he had to spend time in the hospital at Louisville, to have two back vertebrae fused together in a long and painful operation. While he recuperated there, Merton was privileged to hear the latest songs of folk singers Bob Dylan and Joan Baez. We can imagine that someone who had spent much of the last twenty years working in the woods would have a special feeling for the combination of folk and rock that these artists had, and Merton thrilled to the new discovery. He had special praise for Dylan's "The Times They Are a-Changin'." This was what Merton had hoped for for years. He wanted the times to change, and he wanted the Church to become more responsive to the world. A personal question remained, however: How open could Merton himself be to the world?

Merton sought to answer that question while in the hospital.

MERTON AND ZEN BUDDHISM

Zen is a radical form of Buddhism. Zen devotees try to strip away all the thoughts, possessions, and illusions that come between them and the truth. In this way Zen is somewhat like the monastic tradition of Christianity during the Middle Ages, although there is no abbot or bishop who "owns" the truth.

Merton became interested in Zen as early as 1938, during his student days at Columbia University. During the early 1960s, he read a great deal on the subject and corresponded with D.T. Suzuki, the Japanese philosopher who had helped bring Zen to the United States. In 1964, Merton learned that Suzuki was in New York City, but that he could not journey to Gethsemani. Would Merton travel to see him?

Dom James gave his reluctant permission, and Merton went to Manhattan for a three-day visit: It was his first return since 1941. Merton and Suzuki shared a cup of tea. The ninety-four-year-old Suzuki was hard of hearing, but he and Merton nevertheless had an excellent conversation. As they parted, Suzuki attempted to sum up the meaning of their conversation. His words were: "The main thing is love."

Merton was becoming more and more attracted to Eastern ways of thinking. When the chance came to visit the Far East and see the temples and monasteries of ancient Buddhism and Hinduism, he would jump at the opportunity.

He met a pretty black-haired nurse, whom he identified simply as "M," and a lively friendship sprang up between the two of them. He became aware of emotions that had been buried for twenty-five years. Soon he was in love.[60]

Needless to say, there were numerous impediments that interfered with their spending time together. Merton and "M" resorted to all sorts of strategies. Once back at Gethsemani, Merton found all sorts of excuses to use the abbey telephone and to arrange meetings with "M." The most noteworthy of these occurred on May 5, 1966, when, while on a picnic with some friends from the outside world, he used the telephone to connect with "M," who then joined them. Merton's friends were somewhat shocked. They were pleased to see the vigor and happiness that this illicit relationship brought him, but dismayed to think he might be found out and expelled from the monastery. The Merton biographer who explored the depths of this relationship explained that "M" was a pretty girl indeed, but that she was even more to Merton:

> [M] was at last the ideal reader—the Lara, perhaps, to his Yuri. Just as in Pasternak's novel [*Doctor Zhivago*], Lara is the one person to whom Yuri Zhivago can speak freely in a world of bad and lying rhetoric, so [M] was the one person to whom

MERTON AND BOB DYLAN

At first glance, they seem utterly separate from each other. But Merton the monk and Dylan the songwriter had some things in common, including the belief that "The Times They Are a-Changin'."

Thomas Merton first became aware of Bob Dylan in the early 1960s, and in 1966, as he recuperated in the Louisville hospital, Merton heard some of Dylan's songs on records. The two men never met, but several academic studies have been conducted that looked at Merton's thoughts about Bob Dylan. One of those studies concluded that Merton believed Dylan was the modern François Villon (1431–1463), a French songwriter and rabblerouser of the fifteenth century.

Merton felt he could open his whole mind without restraint. His circumstances were quite different from those of Zhivago, yet the same sense of isolation makes the parallel valid.[61]

Merton pondered the intricacies of his situation:

> There is no question that I am in deep. Tuesday (yesterday) M. met me at the doctor's. Appeared in the hall, small, shy, almost defiant, with her long black hair, her gray eyes, her white trench coat. . . . It was a wonderful lunch, so good to be with her. More than ever I saw how much and how instantly and how delicately we respond to each other on every level. I can see why she is scared. I am too. There is a sense of awful, awesome rather, sexual affinity. Of course there can be no hesitations about my position here. I have vows and I must be faithful to them. I told myself that I can and will be, but I have moments of being scared too.[62]

Merton's relationship was discovered. On June 14, 1966, he went to meet Abbot Dom James before the abbot could summon him. Dom James advised Merton that there was only one solution: a complete and quick break from the woman. He inquired whether Merton wanted to marry the girl.

"No! No!" the answer came. Was this true? Neither Merton's journals nor his other writings confirm or deny the answer. Merton soon broke off all contact with "M," whose name was never revealed.

This romantic episode shows us once again the tormented feelings Merton had toward women in general, and young women in particular. Even in his infancy he had experienced very different treatment from women. His mother had both idolized him and sought to mold him into her image of what a boy should be. His adolescence and early twenties had been full of romantic episodes, none of which appears to have produced much real happiness. From the beginning of his life to its end, Merton seems to have felt that happiness in the form of romantic bliss was a forbidden fruit, something to be tasted a few times and quickly put aside.

The torments over the love affair with "M" brought Merton to further thoughts about the meaning of solitude and the conflicts between the active and the passive life:

> The "active life" can in fact be that which is most passive: one is simply driven, carried, batted around, moved. The most desperate illusion and the most common one is just to fling oneself into the mass that is in movement and be carried along with it: to be part of the stream of traffic going nowhere but with a great sense of phony purpose. It is against this that I revolt. Because I revolt, my life at first must take on an aspect of total meaninglessness: the revenge of the social superego.[63]

As the 1960s advanced, Merton became more conscious than ever of the need for social justice organizations and movements. He was deeply concerned about the moral crisis prompted by American involvement in the Vietnam War, and he was keenly aware of the racial tensions that had led to rioting in Los Angeles in 1965. It frustrated Merton that life at Gethsemani went on, apparently untouched by the violence and anger felt all around the United States. The vision of peace, and then of solitude, which he had embraced for about twenty-five years now seemed painfully inappropriate. The removal of one of the blocks to Merton's emerging from solitude came in the form of the retirement of Dom James in December 1967. A new abbot was elected in January 1968 and Merton felt more hope than before. Just the same, he wrote in his journal on January 21, "It is already a hard year and I don't know what else is coming but I have a feeling it is going to be hard all the way and for everybody."[64] Seldom had Merton been more prophetic.

For several years, the United States had been involved in a war in the Southeast Asian nation of Vietnam. The Communist North Vietnamese had invaded South Vietnam, which was supported by the United States, and the American intention was to push the Communists out and to reestablish Vietnam as a democratic republic. At the very beginning of 1968, the Communists began a series of attacks on American encampments in Vietnam; the campaign became known as the Tet offensive (Tet is a Vietnamese holiday that was taking place at the time of the attacks). American hopes that the Vietnam War would soon be won were dashed.

In March, President Lyndon Johnson stepped out of the race for the Democratic presidential nomination. Although Johnson had had some impressive success with his domestic War on Poverty program, the Vietnam morass had dragged him down and made him extremely unpopular.

Then, adding to the unpleasant chain of events for the year, Martin Luther King, Jr., was shot and killed in Memphis, Tennessee, on April 4, 1968. At the time, Merton was out of the hermitage, with friends at a restaurant called Lums, and was able to see the coverage on television:

> The TV was on for the news. Some tanks plowed around in Vietnam, then Martin Luther King appeared—talking the previous night in Memphis. I was impressed by his tenseness and strength. A sort of vague, visual, auditory impression. At almost that very moment he was being killed. We left, and right away on the car radio came the news that he had been shot and taken to the hospital.[65]

Merton had trouble sleeping that night. He recorded in his journal that: "The murder of Martin Luther King lay on the top of the traveling car like an animal, a beast of the apocalypse. It finally confirmed all the apprehensions—the feeling that 1968 is a beast of a year, that things are finally and inexorably spelling themselves out."[66] It had indeed been a terrible year. And more was yet to come.

9

The Great Trip

So I will disappear from view and we
can all have a Coke or something.

—Merton's last public words

E ven before the terrible event of April 1968—the assassina-
tion of Martin Luther King—Merton had begun prepar-
ing for what would be the greatest journey of his life: to
Bangkok and beyond. Even though he had traveled a good
deal as a young man, all of his movements had been in
Europe or America; Cuba was the farthest south he had ever
been. Merton now saw a great opportunity to participate in
the Bangkok Conference, and to break free from the Eurocen-
tric and Amerocentric ideas that he believed had confined
his spirit.

The problem, of course, was that a Trappist monk was
expected to remain on abbey property at all times. Much had
changed in the twenty-six years since Merton had come to
Gethsemani, but this basic idea remained.

Throughout his years at Gethsemani, Merton had been an
expert at finding ways around the rules. He had been a beggar at
times, imploring Dom James to see the merit in something new,
and at times he had simply broken his vows, whether to do
something that might be considered trivial, or to have an affair
with "M" at the Louisville hospital. But now, in 1968, Merton
had a new abbot with whom to deal, and Merton applied all the
pressure he could. He wanted to go to the Far East, to meet
monks and lamas from other religious traditions. The time had
come to break free from the limitations of a strictly Western
form of monasticism.

The new abbot, Flavian Burns, had been one of Merton's
students as a novice. Dom Burns was well disposed toward
Merton. When Merton would approach him with a suggestion
and ask for a decision, the abbot would sometimes reply, "Oh
no, I'm not going to decide. *You* are." [67] Here was someone who
knew Merton's tricks well, but who was also inclined to go
along with them.

In the spring of 1968, life at the abbey showed distinct signs
of relaxation. Merton and other monks were able to enjoy
occasional swims in the lake, and the abbot seemed to favor
more openness in general. By June, Merton had received leave to

go on his trip to Asia, with the proviso that he would search for sites for future monasteries for the Cistercian Order.

On September 9, 1968, Merton recorded his thoughts on the eve of departure:

> It is hard to believe this is my last night at Gethsemani for some time—at least for several months. . . .
>
> I go with a completely open mind. I hope without special illusions. My hope is simply to enjoy the long journey, profit by it, learn, change, perhaps find something or someone who will help me advance in my own spiritual quest.
>
> I am not starting out with a firm plan never to return or with an absolute determination to return at all costs. I do feel there is not much here for me at the moment and that I need to be open to lots of new possibilities. I hope I shall be! But I remain a monk of Gethsemani. Whether or not I will end my days here, I don't know. Perhaps it is not so important. The great thing is to respond perfectly to God's Will in this providential opportunity, whatever it may bring.[68]

The next day he was in the air, headed first for Alaska and then for the Far East.

In 1968, the Western world was in tumult. There were student strikes going on in Paris, a great storm of protest at the Democratic Convention in Chicago, and a general feeling that things were coming apart. For Merton to leave the United States at such a time, some may have believed, was less than propitious.

The importance of the trip for Merton can hardly be overstated. He had spent nearly twenty-seven years at Gethsemani, almost in direct defiance of his own mercurial nature. Merton was by nature a traveler, an explorer, and he had had to do all his exploring from within the abbey walls. Now he was off!

Merton went first to Calcutta, then to the lower reaches of the Himalayan Mountains. He met many monks, both Catholic and Buddhist, and was generally excited by the possibilities of a convergence between Eastern and Western traditions. Long ago he had met and come to know the remarkable Catherine de Hueck, who believed it was her mission to unite the Catholic and Orthodox sects of the Christian Church. Perhaps Merton had similar thoughts regarding Eastern and Western spiritual traditions.

Merton met the Dalai Lama, the spiritual leader of Tibet, in November 1968. The Dalai Lama had been in exile from his homeland for many years, but he remained by far the most important symbol of Tibet to his people. Merton and the Dalai Lama, two men who had led very different lives, nevertheless formed a quick bond of friendship. One thing they shared was a sense of exile. Merton had been essentially homeless during his youth, and the Dalai Lama had been forced to flee Tibet in 1959. The Buddhist leader later remembered the meeting:

> I got a certain feeling I was with a person who had a great desire to learn. So I thought it quite fit, appropriate, to call him a Catholic *Geshe*. This means "a scholar" or "learned one." Also I could say he was a holy man. I don't know the exact Western interpretation of this term *holy*, but from a Buddhist viewpoint a holy person is one who sincerely implements what he knows. That we call *holy*. And, despite his knowledge or his position, lives a very simple way of life and is honest, and respects other people. I found these qualities in Thomas Merton.[69]

For his part, Merton wrote:

> The Dalai Lama is most impressive as a person. He is strong and alert, bigger than I expected (for some reason I thought he would be small). A very solid, energetic, generous, and warm person, very capably trying to handle enormous problems— none of which he mentioned directly. . . . The whole conversation was about religion and philosophy and especially ways of meditation. He said he was glad to see me, had heard a lot about me.[70]

Merton went to Calcutta, where he delivered a paper. Then he was off to Sri Lanka, where he went to see the large Buddha statues at Polonnaruwa. Something happened there that had not occurred in all his years of contemplating Mary, Jesus, and the Christian saints. Merton recorded his impressions:

> Then the silence of the extraordinary faces. The great smiles. Huge and yet subtle. Filled with every possibility, questioning nothing, knowing everything, rejecting nothing, the peace not of emotional resignation but of Madhyamika or sunyata,

THE DALAI LAMA

His birth name is Tenzin Gyatso, but since the age of about four, he has been known as "His Holiness, the Fourteenth Dalai Lama of Tibet." He is the leader of both the Tibetan government and the Tibetan Buddhist religion. To his faithful devotees, he is the closest thing to heaven on Earth.

Born in a remote part of northeastern Tibet, Gyatso was found by a handful of Tibetan Buddhist monks who recognized him as the reincarnation of the deceased Thirteenth Dalai Lama. Gyatso was brought to Lhasa, the spiritual and political capital of Tibet, where he was enthroned as the Dalai Lama, a title that means "teacher whose teaching is as vast as the ocean."

In 1950, Communist China invaded Tibet. For years, Gyatso attempted to find a compromise, but the differences between Maoist China and Buddhist Tibet were too great to be overcome. Gyatso fled his country in 1959 and became an exile, living in India. Even then, in the most dire straits, he always refrained from condemning the Communist Chinese.

Merton and the Dalai Lama met in November 1968. The two were impressed with each other. The Dalai Lama recommended a number of Buddhist texts to the Western monk; for his part, Merton was impressed by the fortitude of the Dalai Lama.

Many years have passed since that meeting. The Dalai Lama remains in exile, and it is believed that more than one million Tibetans who held true to their Buddhist beliefs have lost their lives in the Chinese occupation.

that has seen through every question without trying to discredit anyone or anything—*without refutation*—without establishing some other argument. . . . The thing about all this is that there is no puzzle, no problem, and really no "mystery." All problems are resolved and everything is clear, simply because what matters is clear. The rock, all matter, all life, is charged with dharmakaya [the ultimate body of the Buddha] . . . everything is emptiness and everything is compassion. I don't know when in my life I have ever had such a sense of beauty and spiritual validity running together in one aesthetic illumination. Surely, with Mahabalipuram and Polonnaruwa my Asian pilgrimage has come clear and purified itself.[71]

With the benefit of many years hindsight, we can say that Merton experienced a moment or an hour of "non-dualistic thinking." One of the major differences between the great spiritual traditions of East and West is that Western thinkers—at least since the time of St. Augustine (354–430)—have practiced dualistic thought: Good exists; therefore, evil exists as well. Happy times come; so do sad times. Everything has its opposite, and everyone partakes of the mixture of what is life.

Eastern thought, particularly the type that led to the carving of the great stone Buddhas, is rather different. Eastern thought teaches that everything is present at the same time. That means good and evil do indeed coexist, but they are not flip sides of a coin: They are both present on both sides of the coin; indeed, the two sides of the coin are one and the same.

Merton had come to one of the great turning points of his life. He appears to have flirted with the thought of remaining in the East for some time, perhaps as a hermit. But these were speculations and ruminations; the fact was that he remained a monk of Gethsemani, even though he was eleven thousand miles away from the abbey.

Next, he was off to Bangkok, where he addressed a conference on monastic dialogue. On December 10, 1968, he gave a speech entitled "Marxism and Monastic Perspectives."

Merton had been drawn to Marxist ideas in his youth, but had been repelled by the knowledge of what Communist societies turned out to be in reality. Now he had one last chance to address this issue:

> Christianity and Buddhism alike, then, seek to bring about a transformation of man's consciousness. And instead of starting with matter itself and then moving up to a new structure, in which man will automatically develop a new consciousness, the traditional religions begin with the consciousness of the individual, seek to transform and liberate the truth in each person, with the idea that it will then communicate itself to others. Of course, the man par excellence to whom this task is deputed is the monk. And the Christian monk and the Buddhist monk—in their sort of ideal setting and the ideal way of looking at them—fulfill this role in society.
>
> The monk is a man who has attained, or is about to attain, or seeks to attain, full realization. He dwells in the center of society as one who has attained realization—he knows the score. Not that he has acquired unusual or esoteric information, but he has come to experience the ground of his own being in such a way that he knows the secret of liberation and can somehow or other communicate this to others.[72]

Had Merton himself really reached this point? Was he liberated? His concluding words were:

> I believe that by openness to Buddhism, to Hinduism, and to these great Asian traditions, we stand a wonderful chance of learning more about the potentiality of our own traditions, because they have gone, from the natural point of view, so much deeper into this than we have. The combination of the natural techniques and the graces and the other things that have been manifested in Asia and the Christian liberty of the gospel should bring us all at last to that full and transcendent

liberty which is beyond mere cultural differences and mere externals—and mere this or that.[73]

Merton's last words to his audience were recorded on film. He said, "So I will disappear from view and we can all have a Coke or something." A few hours later, some friends went to Merton's room. They found him dead on the floor.

No one—not even after all these years—has ever conclusively shown what was the cause of Thomas Merton's death. It may have been that he was electrocuted by a large fan in the room, or he may have had a heart attack that caused him to stumble into the fan. The truth has never been proven. In either event, Merton was dead. He died twenty-seven years to the day since he had entered the Abbey of Gethsemani. The date was also significant in its own right: On the same day that Merton died in Bangkok, Karl Barth, the great Protestant theologian, died in Switzerland. Much less has been made of Barth's passing, but the fact is that two of the brightest lights of Christianity left the world on the same day.

10

Merton's Legacy

*The very contradictions in my life are
in some ways signs of God's mercy to me.*

—Thomas Merton

The *New York Times* printed Merton's obituary on page one. On that same page was an equally important obituary of the Protestant theologian Karl Barth. Between them, Merton and Barth had done much to define the twentieth-century legacies of their different religions. Merton's obituary began:

> Thomas Merton, the Trappist monk who spoke from the world of silence to questing millions who sought God, died yesterday in Bangkok, Thailand. He was 53 years old.
>
> Author of an autobiography entitled "The Seven Storey Mountain," which became an immediate best-seller on publication in 1948, he was a writer of singular grace about the City of God and an essayist of penetrating originality on the City of Man.[74]

Into what category does Merton fall? Was he a theologian? A mystic? A contemplative? Or, as he sometimes liked to say, "a simple monk"?

There is no easy way to sum up Merton's life or his writing. During a fairly short life, he authored around sixty books and innumerable articles and essays. He also found the time to experiment with photography and to become proficient at it. What if Thomas Merton had not died in Bangkok? What if he had lived to the ripe age of eighty-five, passing away with the turn of the twenty-first century? Would he have remained a monk? Would he have become even more vocal about social and economic disparities in the United States? Might he have faded away from the public scene, and become less and less important as the years went by?

Many of the same questions have been asked about John Kennedy, who, born in 1917, was very much Merton's contemporary. Because Kennedy came to the presidency at the time when television was rising in importance, most Americans of his time period cannot imagine an old and gray, much less infirm, John Kennedy. Yet these things would surely have happened. Had Kennedy lived, Americans would have had to continually readjust their images of him, and it might have been quite painful to some of them to see their great hero as an old man.

The situation was similar with Thomas Merton, whose readers remembered primarily *The Seven Storey Mountain*. At least two generations of readers—both Catholic and non-Catholic—thrilled to the story of the disillusioned young man who became a monk. But would they have accepted his continued evolution? Would readers have embraced a new Thomas Merton, even if he came out of the monastery?

Though some of his readers and followers would certainly have understood, the conjecture is that Merton might well have been vilified. Here, after all, was the man who had written, "a monk is someone who has given up everything in order to have everything." A writer cannot back away from that kind of statement without losing face.

Merton was caught in a painful bind. He was weary of the abbey and monastic rules, but he hardly knew what life on the outside was like anymore. He was in many ways a prisoner of his own success.

Merton's death, therefore, may actually be seen as a victory for his image. Since he, like John Kennedy, did not have to age or lose his appeal to the public, Merton went out when he was at the "top of his game." His death, especially with its mysterious circumstances, made him more of a legend than ever.

Mercurial is a word that comes close to describing Thomas Merton. He was constantly shifting his interests, opinions, thoughts, and beliefs.

Tormented is an adjective that comes close to describing the first half of Merton's life. He endured tremendous psychological pain in his youth, and enormous guilt over the lover he had abandoned in England and the child he never knew.

Physically tormented is another expression that suits Merton well. He endured one painful experience after another in his fifty-three years of life. He had numerous problems with his teeth, back, and skin; he made more trips to the infirmary and the hospital than any other monk at Gethsemani.

Prolific is also a word that comes readily to mind when speaking of Merton. He was, quite simply, one of the most productive authors ever to wield a pen. He wrote book after book, article after article, and essay after essay, all the while still acting as a monk, priest, and master of novices.

Yet on top of all of these ways to describe Merton is one more: *joyful.* Merton had a great joyfulness, expressed in his youth through high activity, in his student days through pranks, and in middle age through his writing. Time and again, joy shines through the pain of Thomas Merton's life. Even at the lowest of moments, such as when he was battling with Dom James (and losing) or when he despaired for the soul of the world, Merton still felt and expressed joy. This was in his very nature, and he exuded it to the fullest extent possible.

What does it mean to be a monk in the twentieth century? Is there a future for pure monasticism, as it was conceived in the Middle Ages? One wishes that Merton were alive to answer these questions. We can only speculate that, given his nature, he would have delivered complex—and perhaps contradictory—replies.

First, something that is good remains good, despite societal changes. Therefore, there is indeed a future for monasticism. But second, something remains good only if it is useful, and for monasteries to be useful they must have novices. Will there be novices in the future? Again we must conjecture. Merton would likely reply: Yes, there will be novices and monasteries and contemplatives, because they are needed. The world, lost in the busy-ness of movement and desire, needs contemplatives more than ever.

So long as people read, write, and think, and so long as they dream of a better world, Thomas Merton will be remembered. He came to his vocation the hard way, and his was rarely an easy life to live, but he made the most of it. He was quite possibly the most advanced thinker and prolific writer in twentieth-century Catholicism.

APPENDIX

THOMAS MERTON'S PRAYER

MY LORD GOD, I have no idea where I am going. I do not see the road ahead of me. I cannot know for certain where it will end. Nor do I really know myself, and the fact that I think that I am following your will does not mean that I am actually doing so. But I believe that the desire to please you does in fact please you. And I hope I have that desire in all that I am doing. I hope that I will never do anything apart from that desire. And I know that if I do this you will lead me by the right road though I may know nothing about it. Therefore will I trust you always though I may seem to be lost and in the shadow of death. I will not fear, for you are ever with me, and you will never leave me to face my perils alone.

WORKS BY THOMAS MERTON

1944 *Thirty Poems*

1946 *A Man in the Divided Sea*

1948 *The Seven Storey Mountain*

1949 *Seeds of Contemplation; The Tears of the Blind Lions; The Waters of Siloe*

1951 *The Ascent of Truth*

1953 *The Sign of Jonas*

1955 *No Man Is An Island*

1956 *The Living Bread*

1957 *The Silent Life; The Strange Islands*

1958 *Thoughts in Solitude*

1959 *The Secular Journal of Thomas Merton; Selected Poems*

1960 *Disputed Questions; The Wisdom of the Desert*

1961 *The New Man*

1962 *New Seeds of Contemplation*

1964 *Seeds of Destruction*

1965 *Gandhi on Non-Violence; The Way of Chuang Tzu; Seasons of Celebration*

1966 *Raids on the Unspeakable; Conjectures of a Guilty Bystander*

1967 *Mystics and Zen Masters*

1968 *Monks Pond; Cables to the Ace; Faith and Violence; Zen and the Birds of Appetite*

1969 *My Argument with the Gestapo; Contemplative Prayer; The Geography of Lograire*

1971 *Contemplation in a World of Action*

1973 *The Asian Journal of Thomas Merton*

1976 *Ishi Means Man*

1977 *The Monastic Journey; The Collected Poems of Thomas Merton*

1979 *Love and Living*

1980 *The Non-Violent Alternative*

APPENDIX

EXCERPT FROM *THE SEVEN STOREY MOUNTAIN*

"I had come very far to find myself in this blind alley: but the very anguish and helplessness of my position was something to which I rapidly succumbed. And it was my defeat that was to be the occasion of my rescue." . . . It was the end of November. All the days were short and dark.

Finally on the Thursday of that week, in the evening, I suddenly found myself filled with a vivid conviction: "The time has come for me to go and be a Trappist."

It was a strange thing. Mile after mile my desire to be in the monastery increased beyond belief. I was altogether absorbed in that one idea. And yet, paradoxically, mile after mile my indifference increased, and my interior peace. What if they did not receive me? Then I would go to the Army. But surely that would be a disaster? Not at all. If, after all this, I was rejected by the monastery and had to be drafted, it would be quite clear that it was God's will. I had done everything that was in my power, the rest was in His hands. And for all the tremendous and increasing intensity of my desire to be in the cloister, the thought that I might find myself, instead, in an army camp no longer troubled me in the least.

I was free. I had recovered my liberty. I belonged to God, not to myself; and to belong to Him is to be free, free of all the anxieties and worries and sorrows that belong to this earth, and the love of things that are in it. What was the difference between one place and the other, one habit or another, if your life belonged to God, and if you placed yourself completely in His hands? The only thing that mattered was the fact of the sacrifice, the essential dedication of one's self, one's will. The rest was only accidental.

That did not prevent me from praying harder and harder to Christ and the Immaculate Virgin and to my whole private litany, St. Bernard, St. Gregory, St. Joseph, St. John of the Cross, St. Benedict, St. Francis of Assisi, the Little Flower and all the rest to get me by hook or crook into that monastery.

And yet I knew that if God wanted me to go to the army, that would be the better and happier thing. Because there is happiness only where there is coordination with the Truth, the Reality, the Act that underlies and directs all things to their essential and accidental perfections; and that is the will of God. There is only one happiness; to please Him. Only one sorrow, to be displeasing to Him, to refuse Him, to turn away from Him, even in the slightest thing, even in thought, in a half-willed movement in appetite: in these things, and these alone, is sorrow, in so far as they imply separation from Him Who is our life and all our joy. And since God is a Spirit, and infinitely above all matter and all creation, the only complete union possible, between ourselves and Him, is in the order of intention: a union of wills and intellects, in love, charity.

THE TRUE SELF

"It is not humility to insist on being someone that you are not.

It is as much as saying that you know better than God
    who you are and who you ought to be.

How do you expect to arrive at the end of your own journey
    if you take the road to another man's city?

How do you expect to reach your own perfection by leading
    somebody else's life?

His sanctity will never be yours;
    you must have the humility to work out your own salvation
        in a darkness
    where you are absolutely alone . . .

And so it takes heroic humility to be yourself and to be nobody
        but the man,
    or the artist, that God intended you to be.

You will be made to feel that your honesty is only pride.

This is a serious temptation because you can never be sure
    whether you are being true to your true self or only building
        up a defense
    for the false personality that is the creature of your own
        appetite for esteem.

But the greatest humility can be learned from the anguish
    of keeping your balance in such a position:
    of continuing to be yourself without getting tough about it
    and asserting your false self against the false selves of other people."

From: Thomas Merton, *New Seeds of Contemplation*

APPENDIX

FROM WILLIAM H. SHANNON, "THOMAS MERTON: SOMETHING OF A REBEL," *ST. ANTHONY MESSENGER.*

... What I would want to say first is that Merton was so genuinely human. He was real. He detested phoniness and pretense. He said what he thought and tried to mean what he said. In him we find an earnest, genuine, no-holds-barred human being struggling, like the rest of us, to find meaning, seeking to confront the absurdity that life so often appears to be. He knew loneliness, homelessness and alienation. . . .

People were precious to Merton: He respected their uniqueness. One need only read his many letters to see how he makes every effort to identify with others and find common ground on which they can comfortably meet. He was convinced that the ultimate ground in which we all meet is that "Hidden Ground of Love" we call God. God can be named in many ways, yet God always remains mystery that no words of ours can ever grasp. To Merton the name of preference was Mercy. "God," he wrote, "is like a calm sea of mercy" (*Seasons of Celebration*, p. 120). In the wonderful conclusion of *The Sign of Jonas*, he has God speak: "I have always overshadowed Jonas with My mercy. . . . Have you had sight of Me, Jonas My child? Mercy within mercy within mercy" (p. 362). For many people, brought up with the notion of a God who is judge, rewarding and punishing almost unfeelingly, approaching the divine as mystery of mercy can be a source of light and joy. . . .

Thomas Merton has become for many people the person whose writings they turn to for spiritual direction. This is something he did not intend and did not want. He once wrote to a correspondent that he had no disciples. He wanted no disciples. He thought he could be of no help to disciples. Become, he suggested to this correspondent, a disciple of Christ.

Yet, whether he wanted it or not, Thomas Merton, through his many writings, has directed the spiritual journey of so many people whose names we shall never know: people who are in communion with institutional forms of religion and, perhaps most astounding of all, people whose only link with spirituality is the monk who lived in Nelson County, Kentucky, in the Trappist monastery of Gethsemani.

THOMAS MERTON, "NO MAN IS AN ISLAND"

The value of our activity depends almost entirely on the humility to accept ourselves as we are. The reason why we do things so badly is that we are not content to do what we can.

We insist on doing what is not asked of us, because we want to taste the success that belongs to somebody else.

We never discover what it is like to make a success of our own work, because we do not want to undertake any work that is merely proportionate to our powers.

Who is willing to be satisfied with a job that expresses all his limitations? He will accept such work only as a "means of livelihood" while he waits to discover his "true vocation." The world is full of unsuccessful businessmen who will secretly believe they were meant to be artists or writers or actors in the movies."

CHRONOLOGY & TIMELINE

1848   The Priory of Gethsemani was established

1851   Gethsemani became an abbey

1885   John Green Hanning joined Gethsemani

1908   John Green Hanning died at Gethsemani, the first
successful American monk at the abbey

1913   Owen Merton and Ruth Jenkins married in Paris

1915   Thomas Merton born in Prades, France

1916   The family moved to Douglaston, Long Island

1918   Merton's brother, John Paul, born

1938
Merton converts to
Roman Catholicism

1848
Priory of Gethsemani
established

1942
Merton accepted
as a novice at
Gethsemani

1840   1930   1945

1915
Thomas Merton born

1933
Merton enters
Cambridge University

1921	Merton's mother died of stomach cancer
1931	Merton's father died of a brain tumor
1933	Merton entered Clare College at Cambridge University
1934	Merton left Cambridge University and enrolled at Columbia
1935	Gethsemani elected its first American abbot
1936–1937	Merton's maternal grandparents died
1938	Merton converted to the Roman Catholic faith
1939	World War II began

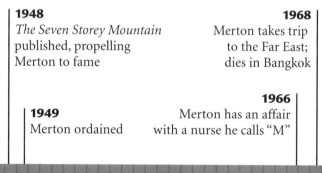

1948
The Seven Storey Mountain published, propelling Merton to fame

1968
Merton takes trip to the Far East; dies in Bangkok

1949
Merton ordained

1966
Merton has an affair with a nurse he calls "M"

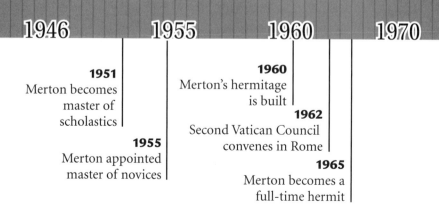

1946   1955   1960   1970

1951
Merton becomes master of scholastics

1960
Merton's hermitage is built

1955
Merton appointed master of novices

1962
Second Vatican Council convenes in Rome

1965
Merton becomes a full-time hermit

CHRONOLOGY

1940   Merton visited Cuba; began teaching at
       St. Bonaventure College

1941   Merton visited Gethsemani at Easter; began to
       work in Harlem with Baroness Catherine de Hueck;
       wrote *Journal of My Escape from the Nazis*; Merton
       left St. Bonaventure and went to Gethsemani

1942   Merton was accepted as a novice at Gethsemani;
       his brother, John Paul, came to Gethsemani and
       converted to Roman Catholicism

1943   John Paul Merton died in a bombing raid

1945   World War II ended

1947   James Fox became "Dom James," the new abbot

1948   *The Seven Storey Mountain* was published by
       Harcourt Brace

1949   Merton was ordained in May; Gethsemani celebrated
       its one-hundredth birthday; Harcourt Brace
       published *The Waters of Siloe*

1950   Merton became the master (instructor) of scholastics

1951   Flavian Burns entered the monastery

1952   *The Sign of Jonas* published

1955   Merton was exhausted and overworked; appointed
       master of novices

1956   The Van Dorens came to Gethsemani; Merton was
       humiliated by Dr. Gregory Zilboorg

1960   John Kennedy elected president (the first Catholic);
       the hermitage was built and Merton spent part of
       each day there

1961   Merton worked on *Conjectures of a Guilty Bystander*;
       began writing about issues of war and peace

1962 The Second Vatican Council convened in Rome; the Cuban Missile Crisis took place

1963 Pope John XXIII died in Rome; John Kennedy assassinated in Dallas

1964 Merton met D.T. Suzuki in New York City

1965 Merton became a full-time hermit

1966 Doubleday published *Conjectures of a Guilty Bystander*; Merton had an operation in Louisville, and an affair with his nurse, known as "M;" Merton was profiled in *Life* magazine

1968 Flavian Burns elected the new abbot; President Lyndon Johnson decided not to seek reelection; Martin Luther King, Jr., was killed in Memphis, Tennessee; Merton embarked on his great trip to the Far East; met the Dalai Lama and other dignitaries; died in Bangkok

NOTES

CHAPTER 1: The Choice

1 Patrick Hart and Jonathan Montaldo, eds., *The Intimate Merton: His Life from His Journals*, San Francisco: Harper San Francisco, 1999, p. 26.
2 Ibid., p. 28.
3 Ibid., p. 37.
4 Thomas Merton, *My Argument with the Gestapo: A Macaronic Journal*, Garden City, NY: Doubleday & Company, 1969, p. 6.
5 Thomas Merton, *The Seven Storey Mountain*, New York: Harcourt, Brace & World, 1948, p. 371.

CHAPTER 2:
From Prades to Cambridge

6 Thomas Merton, *The Seven Storey Mountain*, New York: Harcourt, Brace & World, 1948, p. 3.
7 Monica Furlong, *Merton: A Biography*, San Francisco: Harper & Row Publishers, 1980, p. 5.
8 Merton, *The Seven Storey Mountain*, p. 8.
9 Ibid., pp. 14–15.
10 Paul Wilkes, ed., *Merton By Those Who Knew Him Best*, San Francisco: Harper & Row, 1984, p. 77.
11 Ibid., p. 78.
12 Merton, *The Seven Storey Mountain*, p. 82.
13 Ibid.
14 Ibid.
15 Obituaries, "Mr. Owen Merton," *The London Times*, January 21, 1931, p. 10.
16 Merton, *The Seven Storey Mountain*, pp. 103–104.
17 Ibid., p. 108.
18 Ibid., p. 109.

CHAPTER 3:
Accomplishment and Shame

19 Thomas Merton, *The Seven Storey Mountain*, New York: Harcourt, Brace & World, 1948, p. 118.
20 Michael Mott, *The Seven Mountains of Thomas Merton*, Boston: Houghton Mifflin Company, 1984, p. 84.
21 Merton, *The Seven Storey Mountain*, pp. 139–140.

22 Monica Furlong, *Merton: A Biography*, New York: Harper & Row, Publishers, 1980, p. 70.
23 Merton, *The Seven Storey Mountain*, pp. 225.
24 Furlong, pp. 93–94.
25 Patrick Hart and Jonathan Montaldo, eds., *The Intimate Merton: His Life from His Journals*, San Francisco: Harper San Francisco, 1999, pp. 14–15.

CHAPTER 4:
The Order of Cistercians of the Strict Observance

26 Thomas Merton, *The Waters of Siloe*, New York: Harcourt Brace & Company, 1949, p. 3.
27 Ibid., pp. xxi–xxii.
28 Ibid., p. 10.
29 Ibid., p. 44.
30 Ibid., pp. x–xi.
31 Ibid., pp. 139–140.
32 Ibid.

CHAPTER 5: The Novice

33 Thomas Merton, *The Seven Storey Mountain*, New York: Harcourt, Brace & World, 1948, pp. 381–382.
34 Ibid., p. 399.
35 Thomas Merton, *"Honorable Reader:" Reflections on My Work*, New York: Crossroad, 1989, p. 40.
36 Merton, *The Seven Storey Mountain*, pp. 345–346.
37 Ibid., p. 311.
38 Ibid., p. 135.

CHAPTER 6: Priest and Rebel

39 Patrick Hart and Jonathan Montaldo, eds., *The Intimate Merton: His Life from His Journals*, San Francisco: Harper San Francisco, 1999, p. 63.
40 Paul Wilkes, ed., *Merton By Those Who Knew Him Best*, New York: Harper & Row, 1984, p. 104.
41 Michael Mott, *The Seven Mountains of Thomas Merton*, Boston: Houghton Mifflin Company, 1984, p. 280.
42 Monica Furlong, *Merton: A Biography*, New York: Harper & Row, Publishers, 1980, pp. 225–226.

43 Wilkes, p. 116.

44 Mott, p. 295.

45 Ibid., p. 297.

CHAPTER 7:
The Second Vatican Council

46 Thomas Merton, *Conjectures of a Guilty Bystander*, Garden City, NY: Doubleday, 1966, p. 246.

47 Patrick Hart and Jonathan Montaldo, eds., *The Intimate Merton: His Life from His Journals*, San Francisco: Harper San Francisco, 1999, p. 187.

48 Ibid., p. 198.

49 Ibid., pp. 206–207.

50 Merton, *Conjectures of a Guilty Bystander*, p. 3.

51 Ibid.

52 Ibid., p. 4.

53 Ibid., pp. 23–24.

54 Ibid., p. 177.

55 Ibid., pp. 26–27.

56 Ibid., p. 257.

CHAPTER 8: The Hermit

57 Patrick Hart and Jonathan Montaldo, eds., *The Intimate Merton: His Life from His Journals*, San Francisco: Harper San Francisco, 1999, p. 243.

58 Ibid., pp. 243–244.

59 Ibid., p. 245.

60 Michael Mott, *The Seven Mountains*

of Thomas Merton, Boston: Houghton Mifflin Company, 1984, pp. 435–437.

61 Ibid., pp. 441–442.

62 Hart and Montaldo, pp. 280–281.

63 Ibid., p. 292.

64 Ibid., p. 319.

65 Ibid., p. 322.

66 Ibid., pp. 322–323.

CHAPTER 9: The Great Trip

67 Monica Furlong, *Merton: A Biography*, New York: Harper & Row, 1980, p. 315.

68 Patrick Hart and Jonathan Montaldo, eds., *The Intimate Merton: His Life from His Journals*, San Francisco: Harper San Francisco, 1999, pp. 336–337.

69 Paul Wilkes, ed., *Merton By Those Who Knew Him Best*, New York: Harper & Row, 1984, p. 147.

70 Naomi Burton, Brother Patrick Hart, James Laughlin, eds., *The Asian Journal of Thomas Merton*, New York: New Directions Press, 1968, pp. 100–101.

71 Ibid., pp. 233–236.

72 Ibid., p. 333.

73 Ibid., p. 343.

CHAPTER 10: Merton's Legacy

74 Israel Shenker, "Thomas Merton Is Dead at 53; Monk Wrote of Search for God," *The New York Times*, December 11, 1968, p. 1.

GLOSSARY

abbot—The leader of a monastery; comes from *abbas*, which means "father."

Benedictine—A member of the Order of St. Benedict of Nursia.

bishop—The leader of a diocese.

Buddhism—A leading religion in Asia; founded by the Buddha (Siddhartha Gautama) in the sixth century B.C.

cardinal—A member of the Roman Catholic hierarchy who has the right to vote for a new pope.

choir monk—One of the higher echelons of monks.

Cistercian—A member of the Order of Cistercians, founded in 1098.

confessor—One who receives the confession of another person.

contemplative—One who contemplates.

Dalai Lama—The political and spiritual leader of Tibet.

Dom—Short for *Dominus*, which means "Lord;" applied to the head of a monastery.

guru—A spiritual guide; prominent in Eastern traditions.

Hinduism—The leading religion of India.

lama—Teacher or monk in the Buddhist tradition.

lay monk—One of the lower echelon of monks, who did most of the hard labor in a monastery.

monk—A man who devotes himself to the service of God, but does not usually serve as a priest.

novice—A probationary monk or nun in a religious community prior to taking simple vows.

ordination—The formal process that makes one a priest.

pope—Leader of the Roman Catholic Church.

Rimpoché—Title of many leading monks in Tibetan Buddhism.

Roman Catholic Church—Also called the Universal Church, it comprises those Christians in communion with the pope.

stability—Commitment to a particular monastery and to the monastic life.

theologian—One who studies religious traditions and attempts to interpret them for his or her generation.

Trappist—A member of the Order of Cistercians of the Strict Observance (O.C.S.O.).

vocation—In lay terms, this means the type of work and life to which a person is called; in religious terms, it means specifically a call to be a monk, nun, or priest.

vows—There are preliminary (simple) vows and solemn vows; both are meant to consecrate a monk or nun in his or her vocation.

Zen—A radical form of Buddhism, which believes in stripping away all that is unreal or untrue.

BIBLIOGRAPHY

Albert, Brother John, O.C.S.O. "Ace of Songs—Ace of Freedoms: Thomas Merton and Bob Dylan—II," The *American Benedictine Review*, June 1986: 37: 2: 143–159.

Fesquet, Henri. *The Drama of Vatican II: The Ecumenical Council, June 1962–December 1965*, trans. Bernard Murchland. Random House, 1967.

Furlong, Monica. *Merton: A Biography*. Harper & Row, 1980.

Hart, Patrick, and Jonathan Montaldo, eds. *The Intimate Merton: His Life from His Journals*. Harper San Francisco, 1999.

Lipski, Alexander. *Thomas Merton and Asia: His Quest for Utopia*. Cistercian Publications, 1983.

The London Times. January 21, 1931, obituary of Owen Merton.

McDonnell, Thomas P., ed. *A Thomas Merton Reader*. Doubleday, 1974, 1989.

Merton, Thomas. *Conjectures of a Guilty Bystander*. Doubleday & Company, 1966.

———. *"Honorable Reader:" Reflections on My Work*. Crossroad, 1989.

———. *My Argument with the Gestapo*. Doubleday & Company, 1969.

———. *The Seven Storey Mountain*. Harcourt, Brace & World, 1948.

———. *The Waters of Siloe*. Harcourt Brace and Company, 1949.

Mott, Michael. *The Seven Mountains of Thomas Merton*. Houghton Mifflin Company, 1984.

New York Times. December 11, 1968, obituaries of Thomas Merton and Karl Barth, pp. 1, 42.

Raymond, M., O.C.S.O. *The Man Who Got Even With God: The Life of an American Trappist*. The Bruce Publishing Company, 1941.

Wilkes, Paul, ed. *Merton, By Those Who Knew Him Best*. Harper & Row, 1984.

FURTHER READING

PRIMARY SOURCES

Merton, Thomas. *Conjectures of a Guilty Bystander*. Doubleday, 1966.

———. *Essential Writings*. Orbis, 2000.

———. *The Intimate Merton: His Life from His Journals*. Harper San Francisco, 2001.

———. *My Argument with the Gestapo*. Doubleday & Company, 1969.

———. *The Seven Storey Mountain*. Harcourt, Brace & World, 1948.

———. *The Waters of Siloe*. Harcourt Brace and Company, 1949.

———. *When the Trees Say Nothing: Writings on Nature*. Sorin Books, 2003.

SECONDARY SOURCES

Elie, Paul. *The Life You Save May Be Your Own*. Farrar, Straus & Giroux, 2003.

Furlong, Monica. *Merton: A Biography*. Liguori Publications, 1995.

O'Connell, Patrick F., and Patrick Hart. *The Vision of Thomas Merton*. Ave Maria Press, 2003.

Padovano, Anthony T. *A Retreat with Thomas Merton: Becoming Who We Are*. St. Anthony Messenger Press, 1996.

Shannon, William H. *Silent Lamp: The Thomas Merton Story*. Crossroad/ Herder & Herder, 1994.

Shannon, William H., Christine M. Bochen, and Patrick F. O'Connell. *The Thomas Merton Encyclopedia*. Orbis Books, 2002.

FURTHER READING

WEBSITES

"The Legacy of Thomas Merton," The Abbey of Gethsemani
http://www.monks.org/thomasmerton.html
The home page of the monastery where Thomas Merton spent many years of
his life provides information about its own history and current activities as
well as the life of Thomas Merton.

The Thomas Merton Center and International Thomas Merton Society
http://www.merton.org/
Official repository and archive of Thomas Merton's literary estate, founded
by Merton himself in 1963.

The Thomas Merton Foundation
http://www.mertonfoundation.org/
Provides information, including publications and videos, about the life and
work of Thomas Merton.

The Thomas Merton Society of Great Britain and Ireland
http://www.thomasmertonsociety.org/
Based in England, the Society publishes its own journal, *The Merton Journal*,
and holds conferences and retreats.

INDEX

INDEX

and child out-of-wedlock, 21,
    25-26, 82
as college teacher, 3, 5, 6, 25, 26,
    27
and communism, 42-43, 57, 77-
    79
and conversion to Catholicism,
    3, 24-25
criticism of, 82
and Cuban Missile Crisis, 55-57
and Cuban visit, 26
and Dalai Lama, 75
death of, 79, 81-82
description of, 82-83
and drugs, 21
and early interest in religion,
    18
education of, 14, 15, 16, 20-21,
    22-23, 24, 25, 57
family of, 3, 11-16, 20, 21-22,
    24, 39, 40, 52
and Far East trip, 73-79
and health problems, 23-24, 37,
    41, 47, 66-68, 82
as joyful, 83
legacy of, 81-83
and love affairs, 20-21, 25-26,
    67-70, 73, 82
as mercurial, 82
and mysticism, 43
and nature, 11-12, 58
and non-dualistic thinking, 77
and pacifism, 7, 8
prayer of, 95
and Second Vatican Council,
    55
and social consciousness, 57-59,
    67, 70-71
and spiritual awakenings, 15-16,
    23-27
and surgery, 67-68
teenage years of, 15-18, 20-21,
    69-70
as tormented, 82

as Trappist monk. *See* Gethsemani,
    Order of Trappist monks in
and work in Harlem, 5, 27
and World War II, 7, 8, 40-41,
    42
and writings, 3-4, 5-6, 7, 8, 9,
    13, 40, 41-43, 46, 47, 49, 50,
    51, 57, 59-63, 81, 82, 83
Middle Ages, Merton returning to,
    5, 8, 27.
    See also Gethsemami, Order of
    Trappist monks in
Missouri, Trappists in, 32-33
"Monks' Mound," 32-33
monks/monasticism
    future of, 83
    history of, 5, 29-33
    Merton on, 29
    vows of, 5, 30, 33.
    See also Gethsemani, Order of
    Trappist monks in
Monte Cassino, Italy, abbey at,
    29-30
Mott, Michael, 47-48
Mozart, Wolfgang Amadeus, 59-60
Mussolini, Benito, 24

Native Americans, and Trappists,
    32-33
Nazism, 3, 7, 39
"Neurosis in the Monastic Life,"
    51
New Deal, 24
New Yorker magazine, 3-4
"No Man Is an Island," 102
non-dualistic thinking, and Eastern
    thought, 76-77
novice(s)
    and future, 83
    Merton as, 27, 36-43
    and Merton as master of, 46-47,
    49, 50-51, 61, 65
nurse, Merton's love affair with,
    68-70, 73

INDEX

PICTURE CREDITS

ABOUT THE CONTRIBUTORS

SAMUEL WILLARD CROMPTON teaches history at Holyoke Community College in Massachusetts. Raised a Roman Catholic, he is now a spiritual seeker. He is the author or editor of many books, with titles ranging from *100 Spiritual Leaders Who Shaped World History* to *The Transforming Power of the Printing Press.*

MARTIN E. MARTY is an ordained minister in the Evangelical Lutheran Church and the Fairfax M. Cone Distinguished Service Professor Emeritus at the University of Chicago Divinity School, where he taught for thirty-five years. Marty has served as president of the American Academy of Religion, the American Society of Church History, and the American Catholic Historical Association, and was also a member of two U.S. presidential commissions. He is currently Senior Regent at St. Olaf College in North-field, Minnesota. Marty has written more than fifty books, including the three-volume *Modern American Religion* (University of Chicago Press). His book *Righteous Empire* was a recipient of the National Book Award.